MW00769131

Fourth Printing

TO VALUE THESE YEARS OF PEACE,
WE MUST NEVER FORGET THOSE YEARS OF COURAGE
1941 — 1945

From the author...

In no way could I ever consider myself an author in the true sense, only fate[6] provided material for this book. The result is a personal revelation, and while proper grammar may suffer here and there, I am sure of the historical facts contained herein, as one who was there. We know that professional writers and editors have, at times, altered descriptions of historical events.

Historical events of World War II are what people my age have marked our life calendars by, and always remain a window in our memory. With the realization that within a few years, what is not written will be hearsay, I hoped to leave young Americans more reasons to be proud of their country.

D-Day June 6, 1944 was perhaps the most configurative day of the twentieth century, a victorious day for the whole world. The 50th Anniversary was a glorious tribute and memorial, which literally forced our senior people to remember, and others to learn more about. I will always be very proud to have been a part of it, ...both times.

It is my hope this book will encourage the study of the history of this era, and the knowledge gained will help to ensure a safe and better tomorrow.

Robert L. Williams

---

[6] Fate: Page seventy-seven describes how twelve enemy machine gun bullets in tight pattern went through a leg pocket of my jump suit, missing my leg by less than an inch. Three inches to the right, the bullets probably would have severed my leg above the knee. Isolated in the dark waters, bleeding to death was likely. The reality was, the near miss saved my life-RLW.

WE CANNOT HONOR TOO MUCH, ...OR EVER REPAY THE CONTRIBUTIONS OF THE FALLEN AND FORGOTTON, ...LIVING OR DEAD, OF THE NORMANDY INVASION.

RETURN to NORMANDIE

1944

D-DAY

AIRBORNE

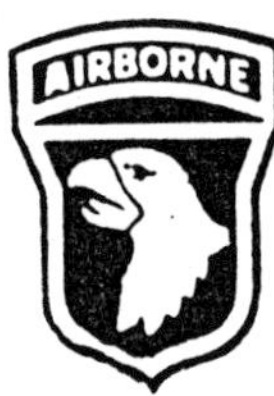

RTN LOGO by Al Gleichmann

AIRBORNE

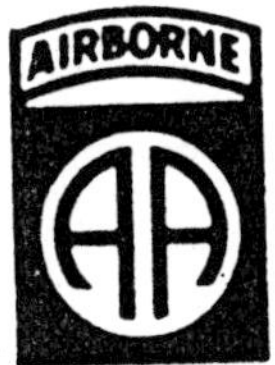

June 5, 1994

SAINTE MERE EGLISE

Return To Normandy

SkySpec
PUBLISHING
Box 75171 Cincinnati, Ohio 45275-0171

Publisher's Cataloging in Publication
(Prepared by Quality Books Inc.)

Williams, Robert L., 1922-
Return To Normandy : still brave at heart / Robert L. Williams.
--1st ed.
p. cm.
Includes bibliographical references and index.
Preassigned LCCN: 96-92321
ISBN 0-9627534-2-4

1.D-Day National Remembrance Day. 2. World War, 1939-1945-Campaigns--France--Normandy--Anniversaries, etc. 3. Normandy (France)--History--Anniversaries--Celebrate. I. Title.

D756.5.N6W55 1996 940.54'2142
QB196-40324

Title: RETURN TO NORMANDY ~ still brave at heart
Normandy, France~~Biographic, Historic, Military WW2
Summary: Robert jumps again on 50th Anniversary--D-Day Memorial

Also Author of COWBOY'S CARAVAN ISBN-0-9627534-0-8

$23.00 U.S. First Edition—Fourth Printing 2002
$29.00 CAN. PRINTED IN U.S.A by Wiedrich Publishing

RETURN TO
NORMANDY

With the RTN Association
Sainte-Mere-Eglise, June 5, 1994

~~~~~~~~~~~~~~~~

By
Robert L. Williams

"Great!... Loved it!... What a story!... And beautifully told."
. . . **Stephen E. Ambrose**, author of ***D-DAY***, *Pegasus Bridge, Band of Brothers, Eisenhower, and many more.*
(Professor of History, Founder/Director of Eisenhower Center, University of New Orleans, La.)

~ ~ ~

"Whatever else you have done with your lives, individually or collectively, there can have been nothing more important and more valuable to your country and your fellow man than your insistent effort to force us all to remember". . . **Ken Ringle,**
staff writer for the Washington Post.

~ ~ ~

"Like the vintage C-47 troop transport that they jumped from, the last of its kind, these men are true classics". . . **Hon. Jim Bunning,**
July 26, 1994 Congressional Record.
~~~~~~~~~~~~~~~~

~ In Memory of Cowboy ~

David Lee Williams

January 7, 1950_____September 29, 1985

Preface

World War II actively began for the United States with the Japanese attack on Pearl Harbor December 7,1941. Since Japan, Germany, and Italy were what we called the Axis Powers trying to dominate the rest of the world, the United States declared war on all three countries, thereby joining England, Canada, Australia, Russia, and the Free French. They were known as the Allies. It was a war of not only our freedom, but survival, the winner take all, and raged on for over three years. Eventually the Allies prepared for an all out invasion somewhere on the European continent. It was decided to strike directly across the English Channel from England into German occupied France. On June 6, 1944 the largest sea, and air invasion the world had ever witnessed was the deciding factor which began to turn the tide of battle in Europe, enabling the Allies to liberate the freedom loving people that had been invaded and dominated by the Fascist Axis powers.

The following pages relates the adventure of a group of old combat paratroopers that returned to France after fifty years to jump again to memorialize their buddies, the men that gave their lives in that invasion for your freedom, and to convey this message to our younger generation in the hope they never forget their country's great history.

............"It is your duty to remember"

Acknowledgments

Let me be the first to stress that my return to Normandy was not a '*one man band*,' but happened only because of the unselfish efforts of the following people.

First of course to my wife Barb, the housewife, the typist, the planner, the boss, sometimes called the little general. To Lupe Gonzales, chief static line instructor of Air Adventures Skydiving, San Diego, who skillfully qualified us old guys in three days, and to all members of that DZ. To Agnes Brunet, Paris television journalist who met us on arriving in San Diego, and was there when we landed in Paris. To Bruce Dunbar and his cameraman, WLKY-TV Louisville, Ky., that tagged along for CBS. John Materise Ch 9, WCPO TV and John Lomax Ch 12 WKRC TV Cincinnati, all very skilled journalist and a pleasure to know. To my long time friend William (Bill) Weathers, assistant editor, and Peggy Kreimer, reporter, of the Kentucky Post for the wonderful coverage before my trip and after. To Gordon Bethune, CEO of Continental Airlines for the wonderful (free) travel service to Europe, and to Max Gurney, RTN member (non-jumper), our travel agent for arrangements. To Colonel Emile Gueguen of La Jolla, and his friend Colonel Pierre Collard of Baron-Sur-Odon, for their work with the French on our behalf and brought it all together. To Richard Mandich our RTN President that worked his butt off to pull all of us together to accomplish this amazing historical event. To the nice lady French Doctor, Bettina Experton for the medical chaperon. To Mr. and Mrs. Didier Louvel, Mr. and Mrs. Andre Mosqueron for the most wonderful French welcome and hospitality. To Don Brooks owner of that gorgeous C-47 jump plane, The D-Day Dakota. To pilot Pat Epps, of Epps Air Service for a great job of flying. To Mademoiselle Isabelle Lebret of the French parachute school at Ferte Gaucher for the loan of 41 parachutes several hundred thousand dollars worth of parachute equipment, as well as the Twin Otter Aircraft. To the French

Association of the Normandy Landings for helping us organize and coordinate our jump. To the US Special Forces in Europe, 'Outstanding!' To Monsieur Rodolphe Rutman of J.P. Morgan Bank, Paris, for sponsor money. To Euro Disney for first class hospitality. To Vernet Tours for the two nice buses that served our needs for five days. To The Honorable Edouard Balladur, Prime Minster of France for forgiving our $17,000 debt for lost parachute equipment. To Todd H. Huvard and Bill DeBrauwer of Southern Aviator for the their story and pictures. To my friends of greater Cincinnati for support and money on my behalf.

Last, but certainly not least, my forty comrades, from the bottom of my heart, I thank you all!

A special thanks to Return To Normandy Association (A non-profit organization) Officers and Executive Committee-

PRESIDENT: Richard F. Mandich
VICE PRESIDENT: Col. Emile Gueguen
VICE PRESIDENT: Max Gurney
VICE PRESIDENT: Kenneth Shaker
EXE. COMMITTEE: R. Case, R. Dussaq, T. Rice, W. Sykes

Bob Williams, Union, Ky. USA

Commentary

WASHINGTON POST STAFF WRITER..........

"What impressed me and so many others about all of you 'anciens' is that you never seemed to lose sight of your mission, even amid the greatest provocation and distraction.

I want you and the others to know that in more than 30 years of interviewing military and political leaders, noted authors, presidents and celebrated thinkers and doers I have never met anyone for whom I have more genuine respect and admiration than I have for the members of the Return To Normandy Association. Whatever else you have done with your lives, individually or collectively, there can have been nothing more important and more valuable to your country and your fellow man than your insistent effort to force us all to remember.

How well you succeeded, I believe, can be seen in the play the Post gave the story. You well know as a subscriber what a short memory the paper has, how infrequently it deals with historical subjects and how cynical its writers and editors are wont to be. It is unheard of for the paper to devote four columns and a picture at the top of the front page to a reenactment. I would love to think that was my story. The truth is, it was yours.

Hopefully you will see in these lines and in the Post story the salute and affection of one who is proud to have been in all of your company, for however brief a time...With warm regards."

Ken Ringle

Return To Normandy

To the editor of the Kentucky Post,

I would like to thank your newspaper, as well as the local television stations for the grand attention they have given my father, Robert L. Williams. As you know, he is the D-Day veteran who re-enacted his jump in Normandy, France, last week. This "Return to Normandy" trip in many ways has become a mark of coming full circle for my dad.

I would like to publicly thank him for his service, not only as his son, but as a citizen of the United States. I would like to think that the media coverage generated by this event has enlightened my generation as to just how important the original D-Day has been to our present way of life. I would encourage all to remember those who made the supreme sacrifice, and to thank those who returned home.

I am very proud of my father for his many accomplishments, but this one may be the greatest of all. I obviously have no memories of World War II; I can only envision the great movie, "The Longest Day" with John Wayne. This visual account of the infantryman on the beaches of Normandy and of the airborne who dropped behind the lines gives my generation some semblance of how it was.

Proudly, I can say that my father has done something that John Wayne never did, and now has done it again.

Jeff Williams
Atlanta, Georgia

The Kentucky Post_____June 15, 1994

PICTURE OF THE YEAR~ Photo by David Burnett/Contact~TIME Magazine June 20, December 26,1994

Contents

D-DAY II
June 5,1994

The following chronology is the result of years of thinking about how much I wanted to go back to Normandy on the fiftieth anniversary of D-DAY, to commemorate the June 6, 1944, Allied invasion on the northern coast of France.

On that occasion, shortly after 0100 hours *(1:00AM)* from plane number forty-eight, carrying seventeen US Army paratroopers, I was the fifth man out the door, and into a country occupied by Nazi Germany for over three years.

Some of you have noticed what looks like a discrepancy in the dates we commemorate, let me explain. We all boarded planes in England on the evening of June 5, '44 but only a comparative few men, called pathfinders landed on French soil at exactly 2307 hours, *(11:07PM)* which the French see as the beginning of the invasion, hence June 5. This trickle was followed by over thirteen thousand men shortly after midnight, June 6.

After the war I had never returned to France, having the usual combat soldier's guilt for having survived the war, preferring to forget everything that happened there half a century ago.

As the years passed, and the fiftieth anniversary approached, my feelings changed, and I did want to return. Not just to visit, but to jump again, a re-enactment if possible from an original 1944 invasion paratrooper's carrier airplane, a Douglas C-47, as a memorial to those that died in the invasion. A large order, but why not? I felt it would be a wonderful thing to do in the memory of those that did not survive to live fifty more years, to experience life and raise a family, as I have done. It would appropriately be the most my buddies and I could do to bring attention to those fallen and forgotten comrades, living and dead, that fought for world freedom. To let their family members know that their loved ones were not forgotten, and to force the rest of the world, especially the younger generation, to know about the sacrifices that were made fifty years ago for their freedom.

It started as just wishful thinking. Then, at a 101st ABN reunion August of 1993 I was told of another member, Richard Mandich of San Diego, that was already working toward a re-enactment jump. We began gathering names of our buddies still healthy, willing and able to go. In spite of the announcement at the reunion that absolutely no old vets be permitted to jump in Normandy on the up coming 50th anniversary, I let it be known that I intended to jump come hell or high water.

For the next year and a half, the Pentagon said no, while our determination grew and more focused on our goal. Retired General Kicklighter, in charge of US participation in D-DAY ceremonies was dead set against us. "Liability and Cost," he said. *(The Defense Department arranged 26 flights to Europe for members of congress, Pentagon officials, their spouses, staff and others to attend the D-DAY anniversary celebration. The air fares alone was $6 million.)*

Richard Mandich applied for and received a tax exempt status for our non profit group called the 'Return to Normandy Association.' This allowed us old guys on Social Security to look for financial help. Our numbers began to grow along with our determination.

Obtaining the help of a former French paratrooper, Colonel Emile Gueguen (Ret), Commander French Legion of Honor, living in San Diego, a city with a large French population that also got behind our efforts to jump again. The Colonel became our liaison to the French official in charge of the Normandy Commemorations Committee and Gen. Kicklighters French counter part.

Emile, deciding to jump with us, contacted a close army buddie that had served with him in Cambodia, Colonel Pierre Collard now living in France near the Caen airport, and only sixty miles from our intended jump site. Colonel Collard was ecstatic about our coming to jump, and he also started to work on the officials involved with the commemoration in his country.

After much infighting among the French, their answer was yes, with three stipulations. All of us were required to have a doctor's approval, three successful practice jumps within six months of D-DAY '94, and get our RTN group to France. The practice jumps were necessay of course, as most of us had not made a jump in fifty years. I am sure the thought had occured to some that we might even change our mind when we got down to it.

Photos: Barb Williams

Air Adventures Skydiving, San Diego, instructor Riggs congratulates Bob on good form.

In February of '94 with the aid of Air Adventures Skydiving, San Diego, California, thirty-three veterans between the ages of 68 and 83 gathered, and completed three successful jumps in two days, ninety nine altogether, using modern ram air square chutes. Lupe Gonzales, our static line instructor spent five hours preaching the do's and don'ts of modern parachuting. A wonderful job, I might add, and resulting in a mutual admiration between the young skydivers and the old timers. The parachute equiptment was the very latest technology in safety.

It was a beautiful sight I will never forget after my chute opened at 3000 feet on a warm sunny morning, facing the blue Pacific Ocean with San Diego Harbor on my right, and the hills of Tijuana, Mexico on my left. I was spell bound by this panorama until I heard the radio in my ear insisting I make a right turn immediately, if I did not want to land over the border into Mexico.

It was a fine show helped along with French TV crews including a good looking girl correspondent *(Agnes)* and local newspaper reporters to tell the world of our intentions. CBS sent Bill Whitaker and camera crew to cover the event with a camera in our jump plane. For some reason they switched planes on me. It was because Dick Falvey, Gorden King and I had qualified together at Ft. Benning in '42, we wanted to jump together again for old times sake. So when Ed Manley came running to get me to go on the CBS plane, I turned him down. I went on to make all three jumps with my buddies. Ed and Rene Dussuq were TV Stars as they jumped and made the CBS News!

That weekend ended with a media blitz and enough exposure to turn the tide of public opinion in our favor, which prompted us to contact Gen. Kicklighter again. He replied that we would get an answer in two weeks. We never did. I believe he was hoping we would go away. Weeks went by and time was getting short. In desperation we sent one of our guys to Washington where he spent a week knocking on doors, among the last was Kicklighters. Our man returned home very dejected saying it did not look too good. With less than two months to go, we pleaded with the Pentagon 'at least get us on the Memorial Program,' and we would use our own plane and parachutes. In other words, lead or get out of the way.

Photo: Barb Williams

Qualifying again after fifty years!
L to R Dick Falvey NY, Bob Williams KY, and Gordon King WI.

I got a call from a Colonel Stuart Chenea, Adjutant, Service Air Command in Germany, offering the use of Army parachutes and ground support personnel to recover chutes if he could get the OK.

It was at a meeting at the White House with General Wayne Downing, Commander in Chief of Special Operations Command Forces, that he was asked for advice from the President about our plans. He replied without hesitation, 'Let them jump.' The President agreed and asked him to do what he could to help our group. General Downing contacted General Kicklighter at the

Pentagon, who was in charge of the American D-Day ceremonies, and offered the services of the Special Forces.

This and growing public pressure prompted the pentagon to put the RTN Association on the D-Day official program. This sounded great, but when our Special Forces in Germany tried to arrange to supply Army Parachutes our government issued orders that no government equipment could be used! However, the ground support would be permitted, and we could be on the program to jump after the active Army at 3:00 P.M. . . Later appropriately changed to 2:00 P.M. at the insistence of the French to allow the old guys to spearhead the summer long celebrations. *(Very appropriate)*

We were very concerned about parachutes, as I had contacted all the friends I knew at skydiving centers in my part of the country and not having much luck. It began to look as it would be every man for himself to borrow a chute and carry it all the way to France and back with our other luggage. I even had a drop zone owner and friend, Bill Scott of Monroe, Ga., agree to go with us to supervise the jump if necessary, but it did not happen that way.

About this time Colonel Gueguen met through his step-daughter a young woman paratrooper that lived in Paris, and was a member of the parachute school at Ferte' Gaucher. As soon as she was apprised of our pressing need for skydiving equipment, she fought single-handedly with extraordinary energy to obtain for us the 41 French civilian parachutes and the Twin Otter aircraft that was used for our jump. God Bless you Mademoiselle Isabelle Labret! Soon after this the Paris Skydiving Center informed us that modern American made square chutes would be ready for us at Caen when we arrived. The same kind we had jumped in San Diego.

Mr. Max Gurney, our travel coordinator received word that Continental Airlines would provide free round trip air fare from anywhere in the country to Paris, with half fares for other family members. *(Just what Barb needed!)*

More good news when we learned that Monsieur Rodolpe (Rudy) Rutman with the J.P. Morgan Bank in Paris, would help with our estimated $150,000 budget. Rudy even went along on one of the buses to serve as guide and interpreter for five days.

Through the efforts of Colonel Pierre Collard of Baron-Sur-Odon the French tour agency Vernet, promised two buses for five days, and would be waiting for us at the airport.

Gen. Kicklighter, reeling from all this pressure of international good will, now agreed we would jump before the regular Army, as spearhead for opening the Commemorative Ceremonies just as we were the spearhead for the invasion D-DAY fifty years before.

For months I had been calling Don Brooks in Douglas Georgia, wanting to know how he was coming along with sponsors to help finance flying his vintage C-47 plane to Normandy for us to jump with. It was built in January 1944 at Oklahoma City, and used in the invasion by the British.

At last, two weeks before our departure he called, and said he was going, that the plane was being painted, complete with WWII invasion stripes, and equipped with jump gear.

. . ..."There it was, suddenly, ...an old C-47 appearing out of nowhere". Bruce Morton, CNN.

It really happened folks, and it was awesome. I have lived the most beautiful and exciting seven days of my 71 years. I awoke on the morning of June 8 at home, from a deep and satisfying sleep.

The problems, uncertainties, and confusion that confronted our efforts for five hectic months suddenly evaporated and were replaced by amazement, happiness, and great satisfaction. Just the realization that I am one of only nineteen men in the world..., the only Kentuckian..., to repeat the D-Day jump from one of the last, and still flying invasion airplanes on the fiftieth anniversary of the greatest land, sea, and air invasion that virtually changed the world. It also was satisfying to realize we had pulled off the best memorial and reminder of D-Day there ever was. The French would be the first to agree to that.

My wife Barb, and I, in jump uniform, left early the morning of June 1 for Louisville, to catch the 10:00AM flight to Houston. Waiting in the terminal was WLKY-TV *(CBS)* anchorman Bruce Dunbar and his camera man, also named Bruce. They announced, to my surprise, they would stick with us all the way to France. Continental Airlines not only gave us veterans free round trip airfare, but told CBS to pick a film crew from every state with a D-Day jumper and receive a free trip.

The Courier-Journal photographer, Keith Williams *(no relation),* took my picture that appeared on the next days front page.

On arrival at Houston, the assemble point for departure, I got a hint of the huge media coverage for the trip. After an effortless baggage check, and a fast pass through customs, all arriving veterans gathered in the Group Room. The excitement of seeing our old buddies and their families, plus the champagne and food provided by the airline made the four hours wait for our Paris flight go very quickly. Bruce got to work with my TV interview, and was followed by a French TV crew, then a mixture of reporters from all over. Shortly after, Bruce nudged me and said we had already been on my local Cincinnati Station, Channel 9 WCPO! I later learned we were on French TV before we got to Paris.

While we were waiting, happily laughting it up, having a big time, the mood in the room changed suddenly. The name of our jump instructor in San Diego, went through the room like a hot wire, shocking everyone when told of an accident that happened in Arizona just a few days before. Lupe and his buddie John O'Hara were performing a parachute jump called a double diamond, when they collided midair. John was killed, and Lupe lost his left leg five inches below the knee, plus many fractures in his right leg.

Despite his terrible misfortune, Lupe told me he watched from his hospital room as we jumped in Normandy.

"There never was a more exciting time in my life then when I saw you Paratroopers on television while I was in intensive care," he wrote. "While I was connected to IV's, heart monitors, respiratory, and heavens knows what else, I pointed to the television making some mumbling sound, trying to tell the nurse, 'I know those guys, they're my friends' as you were jumping in Normandy. The nurse thought I was having a convulsion or something, so she increased my medication, told me to relax, then turned the TV off".

Your friend, Lupe Gonzales

C-8791, D-9485 *(Lic.Ratings)*

One hour before take off we were escorted out on the ramp next to our DC-10 while the Fifth US Army Band played the National Anthem. Paul S. Howell of the Houston Chronicle took our picture as we stood to salute the flag, and it appeared on the following days front page.

As the RTN Veterans sat in the front row, the first to speak was the Hon. Jack Fields, US Representative of Texas, followed by Major General Frank Miller, then the man that received the most applause, Mr. Gordon M. Bethune, President and CEO of Continental Airlines. Houston Councilman, Lloyd Kelley read a proclamation by the Mayor proclaiming June 1, 1994 'Return To Normandy' day in Houston.

Following a red carpet that led to the waiting plane, with the band playing, we climbed the stairs and got aboard. . .what a deal!

The heavily loaded DC-10 took off for Paris at 5:30 PM and a nine hour flight. As we approached the Normandy beaches the pilot announced a ceiling of only three thousand feet and they could not be seen through the overcast. We expressed our disappointment, there upon the engines slowed and we descended to beneath the over cast and at almost idle speed, *(in a DC-10)?* We got a good look at the beaches we would soon return to. This patronizing gesture was omniscient of the days to follow on this trip.

Arrival at Paris brought me to realize the enormities of our 'Return to Normandy.' Our families and other passengers were directed off the plane in normal fashion, while the vets were held back, directed out a side door and down steps to the ramp where we were mobbed by waiting press, and another red carpet. Among those waiting a beautiful girl shouted "Bob!". *(A hug and kiss)* It was Agnes Brunet, a TV personality from Paris that Barb and I spent much time with in San Diego at the qualifying jumps for the French. A band was playing Glenn Miller swing music.

Eventually moving inside, bypassing customs, *(an indication of the importance the French placed on this group of men)*, we entered a large room with more Champagne, food and TV interviews. As the band moved inside and continued to play several of our guys, Bill Priest, Guy Whidden, and Everet Hall grabbed young flight attendants and treated the crowd to real forties jitter-bug. Our volunteer lady French Doctor, Bettina Experton joined in. The French loved it.

Finally someone grabbed a microphone and shouted, "The French are waiting for you, on to the buses!" So they were, we learned as the tour buses stopped in front of the Paris City Building, and we filed inside the two hundred years old stone structure filled with paintings and tapestries. In the center of a Great Room a small man of importance waited to greet us, the Mayor. As it came closer to my turn to greet him I became nervous, as most of our guys were giving him the customary three kisses on the cheek. But not to worry, because as I approached him, he seemed to sense that kissing was not my bag, and we had a nice handshake with a, Bonjour Monsieur. More champagne, more delicious food, and more media people. I might add, this big old

Photo Courtesy: Houston Cronicle

GETTING A JUMP ON HISTORY

That was the caption on this picture taken by Paul S. Howell for the Houston Chronical June 2, 1944 just before we boarded the Continental DC-10. Rollie Duff is nearest the camera, (Killed in Russia May 8, 1995) then R to L, Richard Falvey, Bob Williams, Rene Dussaq (83yr), second row, Warren Wilt and Kelly Stumpus.

beautiful building has only one "John," and used by both men and women. Due to a pressing need we quickly put aside our bashfulness, and used the facilities.

Next stop was Euro Disney where we would stay one night. Here again our group bypassed the lines waiting to check in and received a room key on the way to the elevator, along with a package containing information and free tickets to Disney park, only a short walk from the Sequoia Hotel.

That evening we were invited to see Buffalo Bills Wild West Show. We were still in uniform, so the cowboys wanted a group picture with their horses before the show, which was terrific by the way. The character playing Buffalo Bill, on a beautiful white horse, stopped in the middle of his performance, pointed to our group, bathed in a spot light, to publicly pay his countries respects and thanked us for their freedom. Very moving indeed.

The next morning was spent at the park and it was entertaining to watch the French kids, looking just like American kids enjoying Disney World back home.

At the Sequoia Hotel desk they let me fax all this information *(no charge)* to the Kentucky Post Newspaper as I had promised William Weathers, assistant editor, for his column. It appeared in the next days paper, I learned later on returning home.

In the afternoon, back on the buses, *(provided by Tourisme Vernet for five days and very nice)* for a three hour ride to Caen to meet our host families for the next two nights in the very small village of Baron-Sur-Odon. The one narrow street through town swarmed with French people holding up signs with our names written on them, indicating the family we were to stay with. As I got off the bus I pointed to a lady waving a sign with my name on it. With a big smile she pushed through the crowd toward me. There was no hand shake this time. One, two, three kisses, then I was pulled to where her husband and children were waiting.

Photo: Barb Williams

RTN and cast of Buffalo Bill's Wild West Show, Euro Disney

Luckily he was the quiet type, and settled for just a hand shake. Claudine Louvel spoke a little English but her husband Didier none, which, with my little French made interesting conversation. They and their children, Eric, Thomas and Lea lived in a stone house with walls two feet thick covered with vines. A very nice family, and perfect host.

The small village of about a dozen houses had a school house in the center of town, where the children must have spent weeks making welcome signs that plastered the building, inside and out. Our group gathered here in the evening to hear Mayor Gerard Mahuet read a proclamation and to pin the medal of 'Medaille Du

Jubile', on our uniforms. Each veteran also got a gift of the limited reproduction of "The Moment Of Freedom," by Isaac Jos Bertaux, art director, known as Jos B, mine is number thirty-nine. *(Bill Clinton's is number two...?)* This was followed by a dinner and more speeches and more wine!

The next morning the men took one bus and headed for the Carpiquet Airport, near Caen for briefing and training while the women took the second bus into the city to shop and visit Abby St. Etienne, the one thousand year old church containing the tomb of William The Conqueror. It rained all day and there was much concern about the jump to take place the next day on the 5th. The forecast was still bleak. That afternoon we joined our families at the lovely home of Mayor Col. Pierre Collard for more food and more wine! Pierre and our Col. Gueguen had served together in the French Army, both deserving much credit for our successful memorial jump.

After lunch we were guest of a mock-formal installation, in the rain, of four RTN members in the proudest gastronomic society of Caen, the Golden Order of Tripe Eaters. While few outside France might jump at the chance to eat pieces of stewed cow stomach, our guys brightened at learning that the tripe had been stewed in Calvados, the famous apple brandy of Normandy.

That evening we enjoyed a close family atmosphere with our host, not at all happy with the prospect of leaving for good the next morning.

I awoke about 6:00 AM, peeked out the window and "Voile", the sky was clear and blue, a good indication that it was going to happen. Claudine had a big breakfast ready and waiting. Didier helped me put our bags in his car, then we were driven into the village where one bus was waiting to head for the Airport at 8:00 AM. The street soon filled with the veterans and their host families bidding each other au revoir, but promising to stay in touch. Exchanges of heart felt gratitude came from both sides.

Return To Normandy Association at Caen's Carpiquet Airport June 4, 1994 before jumping the following day at Ste-Mere-Eglise on the 50th Anniversity of the Allied landings, D-Day 1944.

The bus carrying the men headed back to Carpiquet Airport for more training, before drawing the forty-one parachutes that had been repacked overnight for us by our volunteer Special Forces Rangers Jump Masters, that were stationed in Germany. They were assisted by members of the Paris Skydiving School that furnished the parachutes ...AIRBORNE! We had to be ready for takeoff at 1:30 PM. The second bus with the wives and families were not scheduled to leave for the drop zone until 10:00 AM. While they waited, Didier and Claudine took Barb in their car to the airport to look around, but the guards would not let them in the gate. The French military was very nervous about security, that day in particular. Many dignitaries were to come in from other countries that day.

All was not lost however, as Barb did chance to see our C-47 come in for a landing. She poked the camcorder through a link in the fence and got it on film. They then returned to the second bus that was to take the families to Sainte-Mere-Eglise to watch the jump, but did not get very far before it was locked in traffic jam. The driver explained to a Gendarme that his passengers must get to the drop zone in time to see the veterans jump. Due to the official stickers on the front of our buses it did not take long for a bunch of little blue police motorcycles to get the cars blocking the road, out of the way to let the bus through. Then with an escort the families continued on to the drop zone in the marshes of Amfreville near Sainte-Mere-Eglise to await the history making parachute drop we were all waiting for.

We studied the mapped lay out of the large drop zone, during which I worked out a plan to land close to the reviewing stands, and avoid what we were told was a very wet landing area, up to two inches deep in places, due to several days rain. It had small canals, the Meridet River, and railroad tracks ran along one side.

It was about 9:00 AM when I heard the unmistakable sound of big radial engines as a plane taxied past the hanger. As I ran out of the parachute building, there was a beautiful sight. Pat Epps, pilot, Bob Harless, co-pilot, and Don Brooks, plane owner, taxied up in the last original invasion C-47, all painted in W.W.II colors. I greeted Don as he came out of the plane with a big smile and exclamed, "Bob, it was just meant to be." And he had good reason to think so, considering what had happened on their trip, all the way from Douglas, Georgia. We had already heard rumors that the plane lost one engine near Goose Bay, Labrador, and it did. It just so happened that an air service in Oshkosh, Wisconsin miraculously had a spare engine ready to go, and with a turbo prop DC-3, another old plane, headed for Greenland in a matter of hours. They agreed to fly it up to them, and with the extra crew's help, changed engines in eight hours. It was not new, already having 1700 hours on it, but at least it meant finishing the trip. It cost Don $10,000, a bargain, considering Avgas was $8.00 a gallon, $4000. to fill up in Iceland. Don figured they could still make it in time for our jump.

It was ironic and sad to learn eight months later that the DC-3 and crew that helped Don in his time of need was involved in a fatal crash in the Rwanda jungle January '95, while flying food to starving people for the Red Cross.

Time was getting short, and our jump masters, Sgt. Albert Dempsey, Sgt. Carlos Sanchez and Capt. Dave Kanamine (US Army Special Forces Rangers) were anxious to get us in the chutes.

Up to now, we had been clowning, joking with one another, while the press swarmed around. But it was now time to load up, chutes on, the vets changed to a quite serious mood.

First to go on were flotation devices, (in case of deep water landing) then parachutes, helmets, goggles and altimeters.

We boarded the C-47 in reverse order of jump and sat on the floor *(no seats)* on both sides of the plane, twenty-six in all. There would be four sticks with five men each and a fifth stick with six, jumping at six second intervals. I was in the fourth stick and eighteenth man to jump. It was fitting that this vintage aircraft would carry all nineteen veterans of D-Day 1944. It also carried six from other campaigns in 1944 and the veteran French paratrooper from Vietnam, the recipient of six Silver Stars, Colonel Gueguen from San Diego.

We had fifteen men left over that used the other plane, a Twin Otter belonging to a Paris Skydiving club to fly along side our plane. All forty-one ram air (square) parachutes were on loan to us by this club, along with, helmets and altimeters. This equipment alone was worth at least $135,000.!!!!

As Pat Epps revved up the engines of the old plane, the vibrations, sounds, and smells brought back 50 years in a rush of emotion. Because there was no seats in the main body of the C-47, we sat on the floor with our backs to the wall facing each other. We were all looking at one another, our faces expressing both pride and sadness. We each knew the others feeling about what we sensed was going to happen. It is impossible to describe the excitement I felt as the plane left the ground. Sgt. Sanchez standing near the open door asked for and got a rousing 'Airborne', from everybody, the customary pumper-upper before every jump.

It was only sixty miles to the drop zone near Sainte-Mere-Eglise, which happened to be a large marsh area and close to a small hamlet called Amfreville. It wasn't long before Sgt. Sanchez yelled "get ready." The first stick stood up, hooked up, then "stand in the door". With the first man in the door and a tap on the rear and "Go," he was gone. All jumped at six second intervals. The next stick went on the next pass.

Suddenly, the third stick was waved off by our jumpmasters, as our pilot had cheated down on altitude to stay clear of clouds. Coming around again and back to 3400 feet a determined Pat bored a hole in a big white cloud. Nobody on the ground saw that stick exit the airplane.

Then a strange thing happened. The Ranger Officer in charge suddenly announced that we had run out of allotted time and would have to stop jumping. At first, shock, and then anger as we debated to throw him out of the plane and go. It was unthinkable that we had come this far only to drop half of us. Somebody yelled to ask the pilot to contact ground control. Pat Epps, 'that good old Georgia boy,' knew what to do in this situation, and was determined we all were going to jump, no matter what. Pat had written the radio frequency of ground control on his left hand, which he sheepishly wiped off. He called over his shoulder "go ahead and jump, it's okay." He turned it around for the rest of us to jump.

As I stood up and hooked up and moved toward the open door I had no trouble remembering what to do even though it had been exactly fifty years since I had jumped from this type of aircraft. As I shuffled closer to the door I was thinking, that after all these months of uncertainty, hoping it would happen, it was really true, it was now part of history.

When I jumped in 1944, at twenty-one, I did not think of it as history that we were making, I was too young, but, at that moment I felt proud. I felt the comrades we lost fifty years ago would be smiling. I felt the families of those men must be pleased that their loved ones were remembered. I knew I had accomplished something really worth doing.

"Go," and I was out the door, and with good position. The chute opened slowly due to the five foot extension we added to the static line *(for this type of aircraft)*. Below was a peaceful patchwork of farms and small villages. I found myself headed in the right direction with no line twist to worry about. Thirty-four hundred feet below I located the landing area and realized I had to fly into the wind to get there, but things had changed since the last report.

Instead of a twelve mile per hour wind it had increased to gusts of about twenty-five. This makes for a soft landing with square chutes that normally fly forward at twenty-two MPH, but studying the ground I realized I was going backward most of the time. That meant the guys that opened in the wrong direction would be far off the drop zone by the time they got oriented. Rene Dussaq, our 83 year old was one of them. They found him sitting on the church steps in Sainte-Mere-Eglise, two miles away, having a glass of wine with the French. Rene's first language was French so he really had it made. He was right at home.

I landed on the outer edge of the drop zone in wet marsh grass, but felt lucky when I saw where others had landed, in deeper mud and water. I managed a stand up landing close to the railroad tracks, and a small muddy dirt road leading to the crowds of onlookers. My boots went deep into the soft earth, and I could not easily pull them out. Despite the efforts of two young service men that ran to help me, the wind in my chute pulled me backward until I sat down in the tall wet grass. Cows had grazed these fields for hundreds of years and my uniform smelled pretty bad.

As the old veterans jumped and the parachutes came down, the crowd of 30,000 viewers cheered, seeming to sense the improbability of what was taking place before their eyes. The excitement was awesome.

The very last man to jump, Earl Draper, had a partial malfunction due to a bad head down exit causing his left foot to entangle with the risers. Releasing the main, he pulled his reserve. Landing safely, but with a smaller round canopy, he suffered a sprained back. His only complaint later was that he had trouble sitting on a bar stool. He landed only yards away from an aid station where our French Doctor Bettina Experton was standing. Bettina is a good looking women, and I really think Earl was taking advantage of the situation as she rushed over to cuddle him in her arms.

Good thinking Earl. Just to be safe she dispatched him by helicopter to a hospital in Cherbourg.

My wife, Barb, and the other women did not understand what was happening when they saw Earl's main canopy falling to earth. Thinking a man was still with it, Barb's anguish picked up by my camcorder microphone as she filmed it, is painful to listen to. *(She really would miss me, folks.)*

It was over, with all accounted for, and we really had run out of the time slot the Army had given us as I saw the sixteen big C-130's spewing 560 young American and 60 French paratroopers on top of us at 130 MPH from less than nine hundred feet. I remember hoping Pat had gotten our old plane out of the way.

The 'les anciens' *(old guys)* had opened the Memorial festivities that would last all summer in Europe, we were the spear head just like the D-Day Invasion in 1944. Very fitting, and the whole thing was a huge success.

Our group of twenty-six men that jumped from the C-47 broke the record for average age from one airplane, 72.13 years. The ages added together totals 1875 years, spanning time from birth of Christ to after the Civil War!

As I sloshed out of the wet grass, walking alone with decending parachutes in the background, and a proud smile on my face, a high priced photographer, David Burnett, took my picture that later appeared in Time Magazine June 20, 1994, ...center fold, no less! It was clearly *'my field of dreams'*. Again in the December 26 Man Of The Year issue.[1] Another similar picture taken by a French photographer appeared on the front page of the New York Times, and many others across the country on Monday, June 6, 1994.

With a very wet and smelly uniform I walked toward the reviewing stand, then stopped by TV correspondent Bruce Morten

---

[1] Also appeared in TIMES GREAT IMAGES of the 20th CENTURY, 1999.

Photo of Bob just moments after landing, by Pascal Guyot for Agence France-Presse. (Courtesy of AFP)

standing beside a CNN camera crew. He asked if this jump was any different from the last time (44), I replied 'Oh yes, this was a piece of cake.' As I walked away I heard Morton's sardonic laugh as he repeated what I had said, 'a piece of cake.' More questions, more photographers, as I tried to make my way up to where the VIP seats were and where I knew Barb would be waiting. About this time my friend, Bruce Dunbar from Louisville TV and his camera man called me over for another interview. Before long they had our guys surrounded as the news hounds pushed through the rope barriers to get closer. Understandably, regular Army officers were in a huff as order was supposed to be maintained until after the young Army had jumped and the speeches were completed. It was suggested there might have been some jealousy of the attention the old guys were getting.

Several three and four star generals patted me on the back, and moved in close for a picture. One was General Sullivan, Army Chief of Staff. Another was Ranger Lt. Gen. Rutherford, charge of Special Forces in Europe. Also Lt. Gen. Schroeder, our Army Deputy Commander in Chief in Europe. I turned from them as I saw a four star heading my way grinning with congratulations forth coming. This was General Downing, Commander in Chief of all US Special Forces, and the most handsome officer I have ever seen. Naturally Barb moved in close as he put his arm around her for a picture. She still gets giggly when she sees it. A speech, by Congressman Sam Gibbons, of Florida, presenting a first day release of a new D-Day postage stamp did not succeed in getting everyone's attention. He also was a veteran jumper of D-Day 44, but the attraction was the jumping "old guys" of 1994.

Then I got a really big thrill as a man approached and told me he wanted the pen in my pocket, 'that I jumped with' for a souvenir, giving his in return. Anyone who has listened to this man on the radio would instantly recognize California's Congressman B-1 Bomber Bob Dornan, *(Candidate for President '96)* Rush Limbaugh's friend and sometime stand in on the EIB for Rush.

Sainte-Mere-Eglise (Saint Marys Church)

I was speechless as he put his arm around Barb and me, while his wife took a picture with our camera.

Our buses headed for Sainte-Mere-Eglise with police escort and all possible speed as the people in the town square with the famous tenth century church with an American Paratrooper mannequin, depicting John Steel, hanging from the roof was waiting on us.

The mannequin of Private John M. Steele and his parachute has hung from the church roof where he landed, every year for the past fifty years.

(John Steele's exploits were brought to fame in the book and the movie 'The Longest Day,' with John Wayne. Originaly from Metropolis, IL he returned to Sainte-Mere-Eglise after the war where he had a hotel named after him, and became a familiar citizen of that city until his death in 1969 from throat cancer. He jumped with F company, 505 PIR, 82nd Airborne Division in '44, recieved the Bronze Star in 1962.)

This is the only city in France I know of to display both the French and American flags side by side, year around. How our buses got through those narrow streets packed with people without killing somebody was amazing. Signs and flags expressing French gratitude for coming back in 1994 as well as coming the first time were hanging from every building. French school children were on stage in the church yard singing our "Battle Hymn Of The Republic" in English and French that touched me very much. *"Glory, Glory, Hallelujah. His Truth Goes Marching On."* Those kids have no idea how emotional I got as I stood there listening to them. I still do when I view CNN's TV tape.

While this was going on three young American soldiers approached with a camera and asked if I would join them in a picture. With this old guy in the middle, surrounded by three 101st Airborne pathfinders who also had jumped that day, this picture now hangs in the museum at Ft. Campbell, KY.

Everyone wanted autographs that kept us busy until evening when it was time to meet in the big Civic Center and to find our host families. Up to this point we had no idea where we would sleep that night. Entering the center filled with people amid much confusion I located a lady with our name on a sign. It also had my buddie Warren Wilt's name on it. I found she could speak no English, neither could her husband when she insisted on looking for Warren's wife, which he didn't have. After much sign language she understood, then we went to their car and headed out of town again. The husband held up seven fingers and said 'kilometers.' The car pulled into a stone walled courtyard with a house and stable made of stone walls two feet thick, and very old, a farm called 'Bernaville'. Our room was on the second floor and we were surprised to find it was newly done with electric heat. Warren took a smaller room down the hall. Changing to a coverall I headed downstairs with my smelly jump suit over my arm. I indicated to our host that my uniform was filthy from the jump, and that I wanted to wash it. She pulled it out of my hands, insisting on taking charge of it.

Later called to dinner in the large great room *(there were two)* we found my uniform hanging in front of the huge fire place drying, and twelve grinning people, trying without much success, to introduce themselves. We finally decided they were sisters, grandmother, two brothers, and children. Our host's names were Jeanine *(Jà-nean)* and Andre Mosqueron, from Paris, only using the farm as a summer home. *(Some summer home.)* This family was nice, funny, and a bit weird. Jeanine's younger sister Fabienne dressed in black with a man's hat square on a blond head of straight hair, wearing wire rim glasses, would suddenly start playing 'God Bless America' on a trumpet.

We ate and drank many kinds of cheese and wine, including 'Calvadose,' in front of the huge burning fireplace until after midnight. The French got a kick out of Barb when she tried to drink it straight. Hotter then Kentucky moonshine, all eyes were

BOB AND 101ST PATHFINDERS / PHOTO: DON SMITH, FT CAMPBELL, KY

on her, and they roared with laughter as she grabbed her throat. Barb's a good sport, and the French love to joke. It is amazing how ones French improves during the evening with those ingredients.

Returning to the great room in the morning for breakfast, Jeanine was ready with juice, coffee, bread, croissants, eggs and desert. Coffee was served in large round bowls at breakfast and tiny cups at dinner (?).

On June 6, the weather had gone back to overcast and rain as our host drove us to Sainte-Mere-Eglise where our buses were ready to take us to Utah Beach for the memorial ceremonies. With the usual police escort on the narrow roads, we passed through the tiny hamlet of Vierville, where I became very excited as we passed the exact spot Sgt. Benjamin J. Stoney *(A native American with an IQ of 145)* had been killed in front of the old stone church on June 7, 1944. I was just a few feet away as he leaned out around a stone wall to return fire coming from the church steeple, when he was hit full in the face with a burst of machine gun bullets. The night before, Stoney was the forth man out of my plane, I was the fifth.

Vierville has stuck in my mind for fifty years to the point I sometimes wondered if it was only a dream. It appeared unchanged, . . . a lonely place, it had stood still in time.

At the Utah Beach Pavilion the seats were already full and waiting on the Presidents Clinton and Mitterrand. A guard tried to turn us back, but he made the mistake to chase someone else. Barb and I moved straight ahead to the front of the reviewing stand, which was full, except for about twenty reserved seats smack dab in the center of the first three rows. I was still in jump uniform with all the important badges. The place was crawling with secret service people, but my RTN buddie Bob Dunning motioned us to the middle seats in the third row and at the same time tore the names off the back of the seats. These were not cheap folding chairs' folks, but theater seats, red plush! As we sat down we began to chat to the lady sitting in front of us. She joked with Barb as a four star General sat down next to her, whom she introduced as her husband. Another four star with him was looking for his seat, which was next to me, but instead of squeezing through, he asked us to stay put, and he sat on the end after I moved over one. It was the Chairman Joint Chiefs of Staff, Gen. John M. Shalikashvili!

Cheering broke out behind us when Senator Bob Dole appeared, with chants of 'Dole in 96.' *(He was a candidate for President in '96)* I left my seat to shake hands as he put his arm around Barb for a picture. Then not to be out done Senator Lloyd Bentsen appeared, and I shook hands with him on my way back to my seat. He and Secretary of State Christopher sat in the first row just to our right. Lt. Gen. Viccelio, Chief of Protocol, escorting a woman sat down in the first row in front of us. Glancing back at me he got back up with a big smile on his face when he recognized me as a veteran that had jumped the day before, he gave me a thumbs up, which I returned. The lady noticed, where upon he explained about the jump to her. Then she too stood up, turned around with a big smile and began to talk to me. She said "You guys were wonderful yesterday, just wonderful!" I was surprised to find I was talking to Hillary Clinton.

About this time our president and Mr. Mitterrand *(Died January 8, 1996)* were approaching the podium to much booing from the crowd, which consisted mostly of ex-service men. Our video recorder was on and picked this up, but somehow it was absent on the TV Networks tape.(?)

After the speeches President Clinton crossed over the road to almost in front of us. I motioned to Barb for us to get out of there to avoid the gathering crowd, but for some reason I changed my mind and turned toward Clinton. In a few minutes he spotted my uniform and said, "Hey, are you one of those guys that jumped yesterday? You sure are in good shape. We may have to put you back in our army." Yes sir!, I replied *(are you coming too? I thought.)* With that he shook hands and put his arm around me as he faced a photographer for a picture. I have never had good feelings about the guy being president, and I can't explain why I went in his direction. (Bill's 'confession' 8/17/1998 confirmed my opinion)

Both Bill and Hillary Clinton personally invited our group to breakfast at the White House. It was accepted by our RTN president, suggesting Veterans Day. [2]

That afternoon our buses took us to Omaha Beach where I got to talk to Mr. John Eisenhower about his dad a few minutes. He had just unveiled a new statue of 'Ike.' In Colleville Cemetery close by Omaha, I located my buddy's grave among the nine thousand other service men buried there. I had jumped with his picture in my pocket, dedicating my jump to him. Cpl. Joe Slosarczyk had been in my squad and was killed near Carentan on June 13. I held the picture by the cross, while Barb took my picture, and another was taken of us both, by a reporter for the Houston Gazette. Barb's picture, months later, was the cause of Joe's family contacting me for more information. They had believed Joe was missing in action and were very grateful to know what really happened to him.

Joe's grave was a very moving experience for me, but others that said ***"Here rest in honored glory a comrade in arms, known but to God,"*** was very, very sad I remember thinking as I stared at the crosses. An inscription on a small chapel there reads, ***"Think not only of their passing, remember the glory of their spirit."***

Returning to Sainte-Mere-Eglise for the evening banquet given by the French citizens in honor of the American veterans, we were seated with our host family for dinner, with plenty of wine, and a few speeches. A few seats away, was the mayor of a nearby village that leaned over to chat, and tell me the tears ran down his face when he saw the old veteran's parachutes come down the day

---

[2] Eight of our group did show up at the White House November 11th,...I did not.

Photo taken in Swindon, England one month before D-Day 1944 shows Bob on left, with his buddie Joe Slosarczyk, KIA 6/13/44.

before. For a souvenir I gave him one of my pictures, whereupon he took from his pocket a piece of an old parachute he had kept for many years and wrote something on it, then gave it to me. It said *'I thank you for our freedom, Lorence Yoon, Mayor 6.6.1994.'*

Those words accompanied by a firm hand shake was repeated many times by the French. Others said *'Thank you for being here and thank you for coming the first time.'* Sometimes it was a note handed to me by French children.

Our two buses were scheduled to leave the next morning for Paris at 5:00 AM. Jeanine and Andre took us to their home again for the last night in France. I hated to ask Andre to get up at 4:00 AM, but he insisted he did not mind. In fact they both got up and went to the bus with us. We promised to keep in touch just as we did with Claudine and Didier Louvel.

We got to Orly airport just in time for the 11:00 AM flight to Houston. It wasn't long into the ten hour trip before the flight crew become aware of our presence, as our pictures were all over the French newspapers. It was the first and probably only time a pilot of a DC-10 would walk back and ask for my autograph, waving a Paris front page with pictures and the story on it.

As Barb and I walked through the quite Houston Terminal late that night I lamented how my fifteen minutes of fame was about over, but as we passed a news stand she laughed and pointed to my picture on the front page of the New York Times.

It was then back to Louisville and the long term parking. As I paid the thirty-five dollars parking fee, I realized that it was more than I had spent out of pocket on the whole trip.

Driving the eighty dark miles to home thoughts were rambling through my mind as I tried to stay awake, while Barb snoozed, ...rehashing my seven days clutching the brass ring, ...in two days I had met the leaders of our country, indeed the free world,

....totally unexpected, ...how come no one had ever asked to see my passport? . ...It was a fantastic trip! It really was.

Photo: Barb Williams

Mission Accomplished!

I want to recognize and thank three very close friends that have been buddies since about August of 1942, when as volunteers we met at boot camp, qualified parachute training at Ft. Benning, Ga., maneuvers, then combat, and whom I asked to return to Normandy to repeat our jump of fifty years ago. Mr. Richard (Red) Falvey, 72, Hammondsport, NY. and Gordon (Wren) King, 70, Merrill, Wi., Otto (OT) Sykes, 72 Eldorado, AR. (Unable to jump because of health reasons). You guys were beautiful, ...I am glad you didn't get hurt!....... AIRBORNE! Willie

While I may have been the only Kentuckian to return to France and jump again on the 50th Anniversary of the Normandy Invasion, I certainly was not the only Kentuckian that felt the need to do something special to commemorate that occasion and remember fallen comrades.

Mr. Osie Burton, a veteran from Lexington, without a previous jump in fifty years made a parachute jump on June 6, 1994, with the old round type parachute from a Cessna 172 at the Thunder Bird Parachute Club in Richard, Kentucky.

I was especially proud of Osie as he was from the 506 Parachute Infantry Regiment, 101st Airborne Division in WWII, ...my outfit!

The goodies did not end with our successful European trip, however. The fall out continued in a number of unexpected ways to keep the adrenaline going for many months after returning home.

John Materise of WCPO a local TV Station, Channel 9, had loaned Barb a small camcorder to capture some of the more important things on the trip. We were very surprised to learn they planned to use about ten minutes of it on a special Labor Day '94 broadcast, including a piece on Neil Armstrong, the first man on the moon, during the Cincinnati River Fest Celebration, followed by humongous fireworks. It turned out great, and I felt honored, but in all honesty I should not be linked with men like Neil Armstrong!

Everywhere I went people seemed to want to know how I felt when I went 'out the door.' I was never a comfortable explainer, and soon tired of telling the story repeatedly. Realizing the story perhaps, could be better told, and make it easy on myself another way. I printed up 200 copies of a little booklet of twenty pages to hand out to my friends and relatives, that pretty well covered the trip. One of these I sent to the Eisenhower D-Day Center for historical record.

It was not long after that, I received an invitation that literally had me shaking in my boots, worse then any parachute jump. It came by mail from the University of New Orleans. The letter was hand written on school paper, the kind that list all the directors along the left side. The first sentence read, "Great!...Loved it!...What a story!...And beautifully told." It was from Dr. Stephen Ambrose a history professor, founder and first director of the Eisenhower Center Museum, Metropolitan College in New Orleans. He is also the author of D-DAY, Pegasus Bridge, Band of Brothers, Eisenhower, and many more, about eighteen so far.

The Eisenhower Center was holding a Conference on the Battle of the Bulge, May 7-8, 1995. Andy Rooney plus a couple dozen WWII veterans, and C-Span would be there. Could I come, the letters ask, and "tell your story about the Normandy trip and participate otherwise." I could sell my booklet, there would be a big crowd. Then the clincher, "we could cover your airfare and hotel".

What the letter meant was, I would make a speech in front of all those history professors and retired generals. No way Hosea! I had never made a speech in my life. I couldn't do it, and out of the question That was my first reaction, but the idea wouldn't go away. Soon I was talking to Mr. John Beacham, associated with the Dale Carnegie Training School, of whom I was seeking instruction on public speaking. John laughed, and said a course was not necessary to make one speech, and due to the occasion graciously spent two afternoons with me, during which he gave me the confidence to start writing the required twenty-five minute speech.

At the same point in time I had already started improving on the little booklet, My Return To Normandy, as the first batch was about gone. The interest in the RTN group's trip was very high and I really needed to print more to satisfy the demand, and my desire to keep the memory of the heros' of D-Day alive as long as I could.

In an effort to make corrections and add information, I found myself adding not only text, also a few very pertinent pictures that were released to me for a second printing. Soon the number of pages more than doubled. I managed to run off a little more than two thousand second printing booklets before we left for New Orleans.

With a box of the new booklets under my arm May 5, Barb and I checked in at the oldest and grandest hotel in New Orleans, as instructed, the beautiful Fairmont. The next couple of days we spent seeing the sights, very enjoyable as it was our very first trip to that city. Wrapped up in the Riverwalk, Steamboat Row, the French Market and beautiful warm weather, I momentarily forgot that dreaded speech I was going to have to make very soon.

On May 7 during registration we met Dr. Ambrose, and other speakers for the conference. The University Library Book Store had a long table set up in the hall, where I was invited to set up my booklets to sell along side the many Ambrose books and of other famous authors attending. Along side of which, I felt very unnecessary. I don't know how many they sold, but we sold over fifty.

Later we attended an evening with Joseph Heller[3] author of *Catch 22*, and Kurt Vonnegut author of *Slaughterhouse 5*.

May 8 from 7:30 AM till noon we listened to various Military Panelists. At 1:00 PM it was a luncheon with Andy Rooney, of CBS 60 Minutes. At 2:30 PM at Roundtable III, with Dr. Stephen A. Ambrose as moderator, it was my turn. It took all the guts I could muster, but I did it. Using a video camera, I had trained myself to just glance at the beginning of a paragraph to continue without appearing to read it. The reward for this perseverance was a chance meeting later in the lobby with Dr. Ambrose. He had

[3] Joseph Heller died December 1999.

approached me and seemed quite sincere as he told me I made a fine presentation.

With the pressure off and feeling a bit exuberant, we returned to our room to freshen up and call home. The good feelings were brought up short a few minutes later when I retrieved our voice mail from home. A message from Carl Beck in Atlanta informing us of the death of my RTN buddie Rollie Duff, one of the men I had jumped with in Normandy in '94. He had been killed in a jump near Moscow, Russia while celebrating their VE Day, with five other RTN members that had made the trip. I had been invited to go along, and I might have, if not for the letter from Dr. Ambrose.

After that news I could not sit still, and returning to the lobby I saw Mr. Rooney sitting at the bar. I started to tell him about Rollie, but was too late, he had watched it on the evening news, CBS of course. I got the impression he had more to say about the good job CBS did covering the story than about the loss of my friend Rollie. A strange character.

About the time I had left the conference room it had started to rain very hard, with much lightning. It continued to pour the rest of the evening while we attended the last function of the conference, a Banquet and Keynote Addresses.

After the dinner was over, Andy Rooney headed for the airport and home. Due to the heavy rain and water standing on the runways, he learned his flight had been cancelled. When he tried to get a cab back to the hotel, he couldn't find one that would take him. The underpasses had filled with water and the canals were over flowing onto the roads. With no place to go Andy curled up on a bench in the lobby for the night. Pretty rough for a guy in his middle seventies.

New Orleans had over seventeen inches of rain in five hours that evening. It was said to be a record rainfall for the city. *(I reject the idea my speech caused it.*) While our hotel was doing fine, we learned that others much newer had flooded basements that shorted out the power and left them in the dark. We did lose phone service for several hours.

The next morning Barb and I tried to leave the hotel, looking for a place to eat breakfast, only to find the streets curb to curb with water and trash, with all the stores and restaurants closed. Some even had water draining out from under their front doors.

As we re-entered the hotel we were directed to the University Room where the hotel management was setting up a free breakfast for a lot of hungrey people milling around the lobby. It seems this was their policy during an emergency, which the city had officially declared.

Scheduled to fly out at 1:00PM, we were told by Delta not to go to the airport, even if we found transportation, as it remained closed, and flights continued to back up.

As we stepped off the elevator into the lobby we were treated to a forlorn sight that I must admit I enjoyed for some devious reason. Andy Rooney was coming across the lobby toward the elevator, a little wet, dragging his luggage. He looked even more miserable than usual as I held the door open for him. He only grunted as we passed and said good morning. As we hurried off the elevator Barb and I turned to each other in shared amusement. Poor Andy, after spending the night on an airport bench, finally bribed a cab driver to find a way around the water and get him back to the hotel. They made it after a two hour ride, I'm told. Geeze, what a grouch.

Since new guest could not arrive, and we could not leave, the hotel decided we could stay one more night. Being stranded with a lot of celebrities wasn't that bad really. We kept running into them everywhere we went in the hotel and I began to enjoy the familiarity with Steve Ambrose, General Goodpaster and his wife,

Joseph Heller, Kurt Vonnegut, and even Andy Rooney after he took a nap and got something to eat, and a drink in the bar.

Delta was now saying we might get a plane in the afternoon of the following day, which we did and were the last two lucky passengers aboard that flight for Cincinnati.

Good things continued to happen with a letter in the mail from John Beacham, my benefactor in public speaking. Naturally I called him as soon as I arrived home to tell him I thought the speech went well. It wasn't long after that a letter came from John telling of a letter his former Colonel received from his former classmate, General Goodpaster. It read "You should take considerable satisfaction when I tell you that in his return letter to my Colonel he complimented you on your talk. Now you can add a compliment from a four star general to your other list of accomplishments."

The group of men that made up the RTN continued to receive accolades of praise from all quarters, not the least of which was breakfast at the White House. With all of this, there was hardy any mention of Don Brooks and his airplane, or the crew that risked their necks to take it to France.

Since the RTN Executive Committee had made up a number of plaques and presented to our President, the French President, and other helpful individuals that made our trip possible, etc. Brooks was not one of them, but should have been.

I sent a request to the committee to have two more made that we could present to Don Brooks, and our pilot Pat Epps.

Six of us RTN members arranged to meet Don and Pat at Epps Air Service hanger, PDK Atlanta, wearing our jump uniforms to present plaques to two very deserving American citizens.

Nice things continued to happen because of the RTN memorial jump, some expected, some unexpected, like the box of Congressional Records that arrived at my house. The Honorable

Jim Bunning of Kentucky *(Member of baseballs Hall Of Fame)* read a tribute to the spirit of our group into our national records, and wanted each of us to have a copy.

The President of the French Republic, Francois Mitterrand, on behalf of his government sent each of us a huge bronze metal honoring the historic parachute jump of June 5, 1994. It is three inches across, one quarter inch thick, and weighs three quarters of a pound. *(See back cover)* With it came a letter of congratulations on a job (jump) well done from none other then Lt. General Mick Kicklighter and the department of Defense.

Photo: Barb Williams

Pat Epps, Bob Dunning, Don Brooks, Bob Williams, Troy Decker, & Carl Beck....June 95 at PDK Airport, Atlanta.

Each of us received a very special letter from General Wayne A. Downing, Commander in Chief of our Special Forces. He wrote, 'Our officers and NCOs were absolutely thrilled to be involved even in a small way, and thank you for what you have done for us and our country. I always knew it was the right thing to do.'

UNITED STATES SPECIAL OPERATIONS COMMAND

On page V in the front of this book you will notice a letter written by my son Jeff, to the media. I consider it a wonderful, revealing letter about my youngest son, who never seemed to be aware of, or too impressed with things of this sort. With nothing more than a raised eyebrow on occasion, and heard to refer to me as the 'old man' to his peers, this was quite a shock.

Included was an inside joke, as his reference to John Wayne meant more to me than would appear to the reader. The Duke has been my hero for as long as I can remember, from about the time he appeared in the western, 'Stagecoach.' *(Great letter!)*

After running the numbers on ages of the twenty-six men that jumped from the C-47, I found they added up to 1875 years! That spans time from the birth of Christ up pass the US Civil War. Our average age was 72.13 years. I promptly sent this information, manifest names and ages to the Guiness Book of Records where it is on file as a world record.

July 26, 1994 CONGRESSIONAL RECORD E1567

HON. JIM BUNNING

OF KENTUCKY
IN THE HOUSE OF REPRESENTATIVES

Tuesday, July 26, 1994
Mr. BUNNING. Mr. Speaker, last month just inland from the beaches of Normandy, at Ste-Mere-Eglise France, an historic event took place. Nothing like it has ever happened before and it is unlikely that anything like it will ever happen again. I'm speaking of the 19 U.S. paratroopers who parachuted from an aging C-47 to commemorate, in peace time, the D-day jump they made 50 years earlier in the heat of war.

I ask my colleagues to join me, just for a moment, to pay tribute to the spirit of these men who risked their lives 50 years ago to win a war and then made the same jump again this year to remind the Nation and the world of the contributions of their fallen and forgotten colleagues in World War II.

Like the vintage C-47 troop transport that they jumped from--the last of its kind--these men are true classics.

The 19 U.S. army paratroopers who participated in the Normandy invasion and parachuted again during the 1994 D-day commemoration are: Guy Whidden (MD), Carl Beck (GA), Richard Falvey (NY), George Yockum (CA), Troy Decker (NC), Gordon King (WI), Thomas Rice (CA), Rollie Duff (FL), Robert Dunning (GA), Ed Manley (FL), William Galbraith (CA), Robert Williams (KY), Warren Wilt (KS), William Coleman (NC), Richard Case (NV), Arnold Nagle (OH), William Priest (FL), Emmert Parmley (CA), Richard Tedeschi (NY).

US PARATROOPER WWII VETERANS JUNE 5,1994

(26) Jumped C-47 Aircraft

Sainte-Mere-Eglise (Amfreville) FRANCE Static Line 3400ft Atl.

BECK Carl, Atlanta, GA 68 y, 7 m, 14 d,	Nov 21,1925	82nd 501
COLEMAN William,- Banner Elk, NC 70 y, 4 m, 15 d,	Jan 21,1924	101st 506
CASE Richard, Las Vegas, NV 73 y, 6 m, 19 d,	Nov 17,1920	101st 502
DECKER Troy, Connelly Sprs, NC 72 y, 1 m, 21 d,	Apr 15,1922	101st 50
DRAPER Earl, Inverness, FL 70 y, 0 m, 13 d,	May 23,1924	509
DUFF Rollie, Ft. Meyers Beach, FL 77 y, 9 m, 0 d,	Sept 5,1916 ★ May 7, 95	82nd 507
DUNNING Robert, Hartwell, GA 72 y, 9 m, 2 d,	Sept 3,1921	101st 506
DUSSAQ Rene, Encino, CA 83 y, 1 m, 0 d,	May 6,1911 ★ June 5, 96	101st 502
FALVEY Richard, Hammondsport, NY 72 y, 10 m, 3 d,	Aug 2,1921	101st 506
GALBRAITH Bill, Murrieta, CA 70 y, 4 m, 11 d,	Jan 25,1924	101st 506
GUEGUEN Emile, Lajolla,CA 69 y, 3 m, 21 d,	Feb 15,1925	French
KING Gordon, Merrill, WI 70 y, 0 m, 1 d,	June 4,1924	101st 506
MANDICH Richard, San Diego, CA 70 y, 6 m, 19 d,	Dec 17,1924	101st 506
MANLEY Edward, Briney Breezes, FL 72 y, 7 m, 0 d,	Nov 5,1921	101st 502
MASCUCH Rich, Morristown, NJ 74 y, 3 m, 28 d,	Feb 8,1920	551
NAGEL Arnold, Delphos, OH 72 y, 6 m, 6 d,	Nov 29,1921	82nd 505
ONDER John, Edison, NJ 72 y, 3 m, 23 d,	Jan 13,1922	17th 466
PARMLEY Emmert, Antioch, CA 70 y, 11 m, 18 d,	June 18,1923	101st 502
PRIEST Bill, St. Petersburg, FL 70 y, 2 m, 29 d,	Mar 7,1924	101st 506
RICE Tom, San Diego, CA 72 y, 9 m, 21 d,	Aug 15,1921	101st 501
SYKES Bill, Long Beach, CA 68 y, 6 m, 21 d,	Dec 14,1925	6th British
TEDESCHI Richard, Bronx, NY 73 y, 8 m, 3 d,	Sept 28,1921	82nd 505
WHIDDEN Guy, Frederick, MD 70 y, 11 m, 18 d,	June 18,1923	101st 502
WILLIAMS Robert, Union, KY 71 y, 8 m, 3 d,	Sept 28,1922	101st 506
WILT Warren, Abbeyville, KS 71 y, 7 m, 0 d,	Nov 5,1922	82nd 508
YOCHUM George, San Diego, CA 72 y, 0 m, 9 d,	May 27,1922	101st 506

WORLD RECORD FOR AGE ONE LOAD

Average Age 72.13 years...........1875.46 total years.

AIRCRAFT MANIFEST AND ORDER OF JUMPING OF RTN ASSOCIATION WW 2 VETERAN PARATROOPERS NORMANDY FRANCE ON JUNE 5 1994 D-DAY

(ages 68 TO 83)

1944 C-47 TROOP CARRIER 3400' ~ FRENCH TWIN OTTER 3600'

1. - WILLIAM SYKES GB
2. RICHARD MASCUCH NJ
3. * GUY WHIDDEN MD
4. * CARL BECK GA
5. * RICHARD FALVEY NY
6. * GEORGE YOCHUM CA
7. * TROY DECKER NC
8. * GORDON KING WI
9. ^ RENE DUSSAQ CA ★
10. EMILE GUEGUEN FR
11.* THOMAS RICE CA
12.* ROLLIE DUFF FL ★
13. JOHN ONDER NJ
14. RICHARD MANDICH CA
15.* ROBERT DUNNING GA
16.* ED MANLEY FL
17.* WILLIAM GALBRAITH CA
18.* ROBERT WILLIAMS KY
19.* WARREN WILTS KS
20.* WILLIAM COLEMAN NC
21.* RICHARD CASE NV
22.* ARNOLD NAGLE OH
23.* WILLIAM PRIEST FL
24.* EMMERT PARMLEY CA
25.* RICHARD TEDESCHI NY
26. EARL DRAPER FL
27. EVERETT HALL RI
28. JAMES RIZZUTO MI
29. AL SEPULVEDA CA
30. HOWARD GREENBERG OH
31. - FREDERICK BAILEY GB
32. ELSWORTH HARGER MI
33. JOHN DUNN WI
34. WARREN LEVANGIA VT
35. THOMAS ZOUZAS KS
36. KELLY STUMPUS CA
37. LEE HULETT MD ★
38. KEN KASSE OH
39. KEN SHAKER CA
40. ERNEST RAXTOR TX ★
41. DURWARD REYMAN CO

June 5, 1994
SAINTE MERE EGLISE

*** Denotes original nineteen US Normandy jumpers D-day 1944**
- Denotes British jumpers D-day 1944
^ Denotes OSS JEDBURGH TEAM (101st) jumper prior to D-Day 1944
★ Deceased

PHOTO'S: TODD HUVARD/COURTESY OF THE SOUTHERN AVIATOR

PHOTO'S: TODD HUVARD/COURTESY OF THE SOUTHERN AVIATOR

OUR JUMP PLANE TAKING OFF FROM IT'S BASE IN DOUGLAS, GEORGIA FOR THE LONG HOP TO NORMANDY, PAINTED AS IT WAS IN 1944 WHILE IN THE SERVICE OF THE BRITISH RAF. OWNED BY DON BROOKS AVIATION

PHOTO: BILL DE BRAUWER/COURTESY OF THE SOUTHERN AVIATOR

The D-DAY Dakota

This is the story of the C-47A and its return to Normandy as told by Todd H. Huvard, editor of the news magazine, Southern Aviator, as he covered the story while a member of it's crew on the historic trip. (Reprinted in part from Southern Aviator 8/94)

~ ~ ~

Don Brooks has been there and done that. The auto parts distributor from Douglas, GA., has a knack for making big dreams come true.

When Pat Epps launched his quest to dig P-38s out of the Greenland icecaps, Don Brooks was the guy who brought the big ride. The workhorse of the Greenland Expedition Society was N99FS, a C-47A that was converted to a DC-3 by Basler Flight Services in Oshkosh, WI., back in 1986. Familiar to thousands of pilots who have seen it at Oshkosh or Sun 'n Fun, the big red Gooney Bird with its massive skis has carved its own special place in aviation lore. Flying in and out of Kulusuk, Greenland, it ferried men and supplies to the icebound work site without malice.

Brooks, to make sure it was always ready, coerced an irascible Bob Harless into the dual roles of chief pilot and head knuckle buster. Harless, an encyclopedic aviation raconteur, operates Harless Aviation, the FBO at Douglas. Bob has a wallet full of official-looking documents from the FAA for taking care of airplanes. A&P.I-A. Designated Mechanic Examiner. And while most airplanes mechanics have the good sense not to fly airplanes, Harless is also the most feared Designated Pilot Examiner between Live Oak and Waycross.

He also just happened to fly and maintain DC-3s for the old Southern Airways. He is part Gooney Bird.

In less than three weeks, Brooks and Harless faced the task of transforming the big red DC-3 into a nostalgic C-47. Liveried in the olive drab of wartime 1944, the airplane was recast as KG395-a Dakota of the Royal Air Force Transport Command's 46 Group, 48 Squadron, the unit it served on D-Day. Ed Davies supplied Harless with accurate schemes, and the paint was still drying when the plane left for Normandy.

Sitting on the ramps at Epps Aviation in Atlanta, juxtaposed against business jets, the Dakota was resplendent in its invasion stripes-swaths of black and white bands around its wings and fuselage. Invasion stripes were painted on every Allied aircraft flying on D-Day, to allow fighters over-head and gunners below to easily identify friendly aircraft.

Using a 1944 set of shop drawings procured from Lockheed, Harless installed the jump static line inside the cabin to original military specifications.

And Harless installed one new item in the Dakota's panel...a new GPS receiver.

By the time Brooks called me, there was only about a week left to prepare for the trip. Going along would be Brooks, Harless and Epps, along with Joey Hand, Dr. Dan Callahan and Ramsey "Bub" Way. We would also have a German television camera crew aboard, recording the trip for Special TV documentary.

Completing our entourage would be Ed Davies, 60, from Millbrae, CA., an aviation writer and DC-3 historian. Ed had crafted a long history of our Dakota for Flypast magazine in England, and was enthralled at being a part of the mission. Even though he knew every detail of the airplane's history, this was the first time he had seen it.

Joey Hand, 37, is a multi-engine, instrument-rated pilot from Douglas. A long-time friend of Harless and Brooks, he had been to the icecap with the Greenland Expedition. I first met him in

Kulusuk, when he was leaving and I was arriving. We shared a snowy walk to an Eskimo village together.

Hand knows his way around the DC-3, having helped Harless ready the airplane for journeys over the years. Having him along would prove to be crucial.

Dan Callahan, 70, or "Dr. Dan," is a mostly-retired family physician from Macon, GA. One of the principals in the Greenland Expedition Society, he is also very active in Air Force Association-which he serves as its southeastern regional vice president. Dr. Dan served in the Pacific Theater during WWII as a medical technician. He was the flight surgeon for the Greenland expeditions, and on our trip to Europe he would have occasion to pull out his black doctor's bag and issue some potion or salve to several of us.

Ramsey "Bub" Way, 60, owns an automobile dealership in Hawkinsville, GA. He has also been a fixture on trips to the icecap to recover the Lost Squadron P-38. He was one of the few humans who made the long trip down into the 264-foot hole, tethered to the end of a chain hoist. I had done that too, so without knowing anything else about him, I figured he was at least as crazy as the rest of the guys.

You've read those long stories in aviation magazines about the trials and tribulations of ferry pilots braving the North Atlantic to shepherd their craft to Europe. You know about the complicated logistical planning for such flights, figuring fuel burns and installing ferry tanks. Survival techniques and mastery over the weather. Countless hours spent carefully checking their routes and stuff like that.Right?

Epps doesn't do it quite that way. The extent of his planning is remembering to ask his patient wife Ann to make sure he has some extra underwear. He flies to Greenland like most people go down to the corner market for a gallon of milk.

The day we left, he was working in his corner office overlooking the runways at DeKalb-Peachtree Airport. When it got dark, it dawned on him that he needed to pack. Ann packed his clothes, I'm sure, because all Pat thought to bring was his bicycle.

With the passenger manifest set we were all assembled in Atlanta, scurrying around to take care of last-minute details. My friend Bob Minter from Nashville was in Atlanta on business, and he stuck around until late in the evening to see us off. He hauled me to a grocery store, where I stocked up on critical items like Oreos and Snapple. Everyone brought food, and like an airborne smorgasbord, we had boxes of stuff to eat and drink on the long flights.

Finally, at 1:45a.m., we closed the doors and rumbled down runway 2 at PDK. Next stop, Quebec City, Canada.

During the seven hour flight to Quebec, the heated cockpit provided the only warmth in the airplane. Joey Hand had managed to curl up his large frame on the floor while Harless, slightly built, contorted his lanky frame into the cramped navigator's seat and tried to doze.

The Dakota droned on. Epps, flying from the left seat, seemed to actually be a part of the equipment rather than a manipulator of it.

In the back of the cold cargo hold, six old airline seats had been secured to the floor tracks. The others had fallen into restless sleep, exhausted already from the long day of preparation.

The airplane was at 7,000 feet, churning along through the clouds of a cold front over the Northeast. Brooks, in the right seat, spoke over the intercom to Epps, "How cold do you think it is out there?"

"Warm," Epps drawled, and a moment later pondered, "Don't you think it's warm?"

And a few seconds later he added, "Keep an eye out there for ice."

Don looked over at him and dryly responded, "If I start talking like Barney Fife, there's ice."

On through the front and into a brilliant dawn, the sunrise poured a soft light over the invasion stripes on the Dakota's wings. Below us, the St Lawrence Seaway arced across our path as we descended to land at Quebec.

Notorious for oil leaks, big radials like the Dakota's Pratt & Whitney R-1830 Twin Wasps often leave pools of fluid beneath their cowls. On the ground at Quebec, though, Harless seemed concerned. There was a lot of oil, more than normal, and it was all over the right engine and gear well.

After some tinkering and figuring, he and Hand set about removing the entire right engine cowling to get a better look. Working out of a red toolbox, the two took on the profiles of shade tree mechanics on the ramp of Quebec's government hangars.

Five hours later, it was decided that the leaks were under control and we could still make Goose Bay, four hours north. The weather had been good over the north that day, and Epps had hoped to push on to Greenland. The long delay at Quebec nixed that goal, so a night at Goose Bay would be in order.

I had been to Greenland before with these yahoos, so I had an idea of what to expect. I had gone out and bought some more Arctic gear, for the ride north in the cargo bay of the Dakota would be frigid.

The ride was noisy, and the wind blew in from under the edges of the cargo door. We would use heavy gray duct tape to seal the door and keep the freezing wind out. Still,at 9,000 feet the temperature inside the cabin would be as low as zero degrees Fahrenheit.

Layers of clothes and a wool blanket made the ride bearable. I fashioned a bed atop the netted cargo that took up the length of the cabin and tried to sleep.

Back at Douglas, with the knowledge that "if ya gotta go, ya gotta go," I had constructed a temporary john from a large, round planter. I attached a toilet seat and used kitchen trash bags to complete the sanitary system. Through good planning or sheer determination, none of us had to brave the cold in an effort to use my handsome can. A five-gallon can with a large funnel provided us with a relief tube. All the comforts of home.

Brooks stepped into the cabin and knelt to peer out the window at the right engine. He grimaced. The engine cowl had a growing stream of oil spilling into the slip-stream. In a few minutes, the whole cowling would be blanketed in oil. Oil from the engine. The engine oil.

Below, there was absolutely nowhere for a Gooney Bird to land among the rocky crags and wooded hills of the inhospitable Labrador coast.

"Do you want to land in the rocks or one of those lakes?" Epps asked Harless.

"Pat, I want to land at Goose Bay," Harless said stoically.

We were welcomed to Goose Bay by the entire base fire brigade. There was no fire-in fact, the sturdy radial engine continued to develop power and hold oil pressure, even though it turned out that one cylinder had blown and another was cracked.

We crowded under the engine, which was covered unceremoniously in oil, to inspect the damage and congratulate ourselves on having lived through the ordeal.

Harless pulled himself up on the front of the cowling to peer into the engine, and saw the cracked jug. I had broken the prop control cable bracket, which could have presented real problems if we'd had to feather the prop.

We left the airplane on the ramp and warmed up inside at Woodard Aviation Services, the FBO at Goose Bay. Murray Pike, the manager, would provide us with tremendous help over the next few days.

That night at dinner, we did what any group of pilots should do in such a situation. Drank Scotch.

I had the foresight to bring along a fifth of Johnny Walker Black Label. We poured shots from the bottle and raised a toast to Epps and Harless.

Thoughts of taking the airplane over the ocean on the next leg were on everyone's mind, but there was outward determination to continue. Going back now was not an option.

"We have a mission to complete, and that's what we're going to do," Brooks said. "We're expected . Folks are waiting on us."

With that said, the task of fixing or replacing the engine became the focus.

Epps called Warren Basler. Basler Flight Services, Inc. is known for its specialty of renovating DC-3s, and had rebuilt Brooks plane in 1986-converting it from a C-47 to a DC-3. They knew the airplane as Big Red for its distinctive paint scheme when it flew with the Greenland Expedition.

Basler told Epps that they kept a couple of engines on hand to be used for ferrying in DC-3s from around the world. These spares, called QECs for Quick Engine Change, were already built up with wiring, hoses and accessories. In theory, you simply unbolt the bad engine from its mounts and stick the QEC in its place, tighten a few hoses and off you fly.

As fate...or just dumb luck...would have it, Basler happened to have one of his turbine conversion DC-3s in Oshkosh, scheduled to fly to Germany. Incredibly, the plane would be leaving for Goose Bay within hours of Epp's call. Basler would put an engine in the turbine DC-3 and it would be delivered to us at Goose. We would have a good engine for the Dakota in a matter of hours.

By the time the Basler turbine rolled out on Runway 6 at Goose about 11 p.m., a cold rain was beginning to fall. In sharp contrast to our 140-knot groundspeed on the way to Goose Bay, Basler pilot Dan Reid tracked better than 300 knots in the turbine Gooney.

Goose Bay has been a way point for aircraft crossing the Atlantic for many decades. Until 1992 the United States Air Force maintained a large base, when the war reserve of fuel was largely burned away during Desert Storm.

Since that time, it has become a training facility for NATO operations hosted by the Canadian Air Force. Contingents from several air forces maintain a presence for the base's NATO mission of training fighter pilots to fly low-level, high-speed flights. While we were at Goose, the German Luftwaffe had a squadron each of F-4 Phantoms and Tornadoes, the Royal Air Force had two squadrons of Tornadoes and Jaguars and the Dutch were flying F-16s. All day long, the base was ringing with the tremendous noise of fighters taking off and returning.

The Royal Air Force allowed us to use one of their large heated hangers, a real plus in the 35-knot wind that was raking the ramp. The airplane, after all, was wearing its original R.A.F. colors.

R.A.F. Hanger 6 at Goose Bay looms like a concrete dinosaur over the vast ramp. Great doors grudgingly lumber on their tracks. slowly revealing a cavernous space four or five stories tall and a couple of hundred feet long and deep. British airman and technicians go about their daily tasks of maintaining fighters and supplies for the outpost.

With no tug equipped to move the Dakota, Harless and Hand struggled to steer the tailwheel with a 20-foot-long steel towbar. The sight of the Dakota trundling along the taxiway, with grown men chasing after it in an attemp to herd it along, must have appeared comical to the Luffwaffe F-4 pilots rolling past to their ramp.

When the Basler turbine pulled up to the hanger the next morning, Joey Hand deftly maneuvered a large forklift into position, and after a few minutes of cautious finagling, the replacement engine was sitting next to the C-47. The task of accomplishing the engine change was ready to begin in earnest.

Harless and Brooks exchanged grimaces as they looked over the new radial powerplant. The QEC engine had higher time on it than Harless expected (1700hrs)... and, as would normally be the case, many of the fittings and accessories would have to be changed or altered to work on our Dakota. The back end had some broken connectors and wires, and a few other differences were noted that would require extra effort to get the engine ready for hanging on the right wing.

For the next four days, the big hanger would be our home while Harless, Hand and Brooks struggled to replace an engine with minimal equipment.

Everyone pitched in to help where they could. Doc Callahan became proficient at spreading and shoveling oil-dry. Davies and I became scroungers, visting tool sheds and mechanic's bays in the RAF's and Luffwaffe hangers to find screws and bolts and knick-knack parts that Harless needed. Bub Way went to work with a wrench to dissemble hoses and accessories from the old engine.

When the work was finally finished, the weather over Greenland had deteriorated. Pat made several trips to the Candian Forces Weather Office and called contacts in Narsarsuaq, Greenland, to get first-hand reports. All of our possible landing sites in Greenland...Godthab, Sonde Stromford and Narsarsuaq... were marginal, with low ceilings and high winds. The threat of icing was great. When the weather failed to improve over several hours, he decided to wait.

Here was where his experience in flying to Greenland over the last ten years shone through. While other ferry pilots were agonizing about the conditions, Epps had gone to sleep. Conditions did not need to be perfect for him, though.

"If you wait for it to be perfect up here, you'll never go anywhere," he observed.

It worked out, for everyone was tired and Harless was a zombie. He slep most of the day, arising now and then only to eat.

At 4:30 a.m., Epps popped out of bed like hot toast from a toaster. At this time of year this far north, the sun was already up, brightly shinning through a crystal-clear sky. The nasty cold overcast had evaporated over Narsarsuaq, known during WWII as BW-1.

We filled a couple of thermoses with steaming coffee, cranked the engines and took off, glad to be on our way. Epps turned northeast, flying low along the banks of the Churchill River to give the good folks of Goose Bay-Happy Valley a fond farewell.

The new engine hummed along, and with each mile, our confidence and spirits were raised. With favorable winds blowing us along, the Dakota made 180 knots ground speed, shortening the trip to Narsarsuaq to four hours.

Pat flew 50 miles up a fjord to the airfield, buzzing along at a couple of hundred feet. The clarity of the air in Greenland gives everything below a vivid color. Ice floes and small icebergs floated in the dark blue water of the fjord. Waterfalls cascaded into the river below from stark, rocky cliffs lining its banks. Now and again, a single house or a small isolated village clung to low, flat ground by the water.

The scenery is great going into Narsarsuaq for a landing. But the thrill fades quickly if you're the guy paying the gas bill for a C-47. One hour and $4,000 worth of $8-per-gallon avgas later we were climbing out of the airstrip, flying up a glacier to gain altitude for the flight to Reykjavik, Iceland.

We had hoped to fly to Kulusuk, farther north and the staging center for the Greenland Expedition's operations on the ice cap. Brooks had stowed away some international contraband....2,000 rounds of 7 mm ammunition smuggled in an ice cooler... for local friends in Kulusuk who needed it for hunting. Since we weren't going to make it, the Commissioner of Civil Aviation in Narsarsuaq would deliver it for us.

Reykjavik, Iceland, is a terrific, modern city. The people are friendly and engaging, speak English and like Americans. We were met on the ramp by Gunnar Thorsteinsson, an official with the Iceland Civil Aviation Administration. Gunnar had arranged hotel accommodations for us and had the local media out in force to greet us. A long day of flying had been rewarded with fine Icelandic fish for dinner and a welcome night of rest.

The next morning we made the four-hour hop down to Glasgow, Scotland, where we landed for fuel and to clear British customs. We had touched down in our fourth country and, so far, hadn't had to show our passports to anyone.

During the long flights across the Atlantic, Epps and Harless would leave their seats to relax or doze. I took advantage of the opportunity to fly the Dakota for an hour or so at a time. I'm not sure how much DC-3 time goes for, but I sure enjoyed my five or six hours worth of it. Even flying the thing straight and level, following a heading, was huge fun. It flies big and heavy, but friendly.

On the way to Glasgow, I was flying when it was time to give a position report. Standard procedure on international overwater flights, the position report is used in non-radar environments.

Its standard sequence is position, time, altitude, estimated time over the next fix and then the following fix. At 9,000 feet, I could not raise Iceland control on the radio, so I simply broadcast. "Any station or aircraft hearing this transmission, respond," I keyed.

An airliner tens of thousands of feet above answered, and passed our report on to Iceland.

Below, the ocean bent away in all directions.

By seven o'clock that night, we were sitting in the pub of the Babbity Bowster, a quaint inn Epps knew of in Glasgow's Merchant City district. The apparent proprietor wore an eye patch, and the waitress was a cherry redhead by the name of Judy. After several quick Scotches and at least a few pints of the local bitters, we were getting into our cups as we celebrated the successful crossing.

Brooks looked over at me and said, "Before we started, you asked me how dangerous it would be." Then, releasing a relieved belly laugh, he answered. "It's real damn dangerous, that's how dangerous."

The Babbity Bowster provided a good night's sleep, and the next morning we loaded up and flew to R.A.F. Mildenhall north of London to collect information on our flights to France. We had been expected at Mildenhall several days earlier to take part in a grand airshow, but the blown engine made us miss it. Instead, we would head on down to Duxford for a couple of days.

Steven Gray is an Englishman who has preserved the history of WWII fighters like no other man. His operation, called The Fighter Collection, is located in a WWII hangar at Duxford. The Duxford aerodrome is home to the Imperial War Museum's aviation collection, which is housed along-side the famous turf runways where Spitfires rose to meet the Luftwaffe during the Battle of Britian. Now the museum, along with Gray's collection, is an immensely popular attraction where daily flights of vintage fighters thrill visitors.

Gray's collection sports one of just about every fighter of WWII. Spitfires, Hurricanes, Mustangs. He has a Wildcat, Hellcat, and a Bearcat, along with a Sea Fury, P-38, P-40, and more. All of the airplanes are flown regularly, performing spontaneous daredevilry over the museum grounds.

Gray met us when we landed and arranged accommodations for our crew at nearby Cambridge. Harless was quickly becoming adept at finding pubs, and he headed us at one called The Eagle. The pub is famous for its back room, where its ceiling still bears the imprint of young airmen 50 years past. They would come in at night to drink and relax, and somehow started a tradition of using candles or lighters to inscribe the names of their squadrons on the ceiling of the pub. Their missions are still plain to read today, and gave a ghostly quality to the evening's banter.

On June 3 we were scheduled to fly to Caen, France, for a rehearsal flight over the Sainte-Mere-Eglise drop zone. Pat had jumped through several hoops during the day to make the flight go off. He had to get air traffic control at Duxford to grant permission for an early take-off; we would have to be wheels-up by 6 a.m. to make our arrival time of 9 a.m. local at Caen. He had filed a flight plan with Stansted Airport ATC, and everything looked hunky-dory.

But the sage of our group's efforts to get the Dakota to France was not yet over. Late that night, after another good evening of food and several more pints of bitters, an ominous note had been slipped under our hotel room door.

Stansted had received a telex from Caen. Our flight plan had been turned away.

"This message from Caen this evening following refusal to accept your flight despite a signal from us stating that your flight was connected with the D-Day ceremonies.

"Madame LeMardis, director of Caen Airport, confirms that we cannot accept N99FS tomorrow, as the authorization has not been requested yesterday or before."

The note said we could call her after 7 a.m. the next day, too late to meet our Air Force contacts.

Epps was irritated. "The whole thing about so much security is ridiculous," he muttered.

Brooks wasn't happy either. "I'm not surprised. There are a lot of people that didn't want the jump to happen all along. I expected some sort of red tape to show up," he muttered. "But we could have quit any number of times. We just won't quit now."

Epps remembered that he had not included our Air Force-issued call sign_Victory_in our flight plan, nor our diplomatic code. He called Stansted back, and asked them to refile with the missing information. The plan was still on to take off, and hope that in the morning something good would happen over in Caen.

Eisenhower, it seemed, had less trouble getting to Normandy than we were having.

Crossing the English Channel the next day was unforgettable. Flying over the white cliffs of Dover, I imagined what the scene below would have looked like 50 years ago. Just a few short minutes ahead lay the Normandy coastline, and I thought about what it would have been like to be in this airplane on a fateful ride into combat.

We crossed the coast and looked down on Utah Beach and the green fields beyond. It was a peaceful patchwork of farms and small villages. How did it look in June 1944?

We reached Caen to find it an airport besieged by an international military machine. Several air forces were to be involved in the upcoming D-Day events, and it looked like more logistical planning was going into the commemoration than did the original invasion. We were met by ranking officers of both the Air Force and the Army, and several Special Forces Rangers were assigned to our plane as jumpmasters. We took the Dakota up for a dry run over the drop zone while the Rangers inspected the static line and got a feel for the jump.

We had planned to fly back to England, but decided to linger in the port of Le Havre, 50 miles north of Caen. The ramp at Le Havre included a B-17, a B-25, three C-47s and two or three Mustangs. The assembled fleet of airplanes, including ours, would take part in a formation fly-over of the fifteen heads of state, including President Bill Clinton and Queen Elizabeth II, who would take part in ceremonies June 6 at Omaha Beach.

The most remarkable part of our adventure was the weather in Normandy on June 4. Almost duplicating the bad weather that plagued Eisenhower's decision on the invasion, the ceiling was low and dark. Winds with gusts to 40 or 50 knots blew cold rain in horizontal stilettos. If the weather didn't change, there would be no jump. Conditions set by the Army held that the ceiling had to be high enough to put the jumpers out 3400 feet, no lower, and the surface winds could not exceed 13 knots.

June 5 dawned with bright sunshine and blue skies, dotted with occasional cumulus about 3,000 feet. The wicked weather of the night before had passed somehow, and the winds had quieted. There would be a jump today.

We landed at Caen again, and before the door could be opened several of the D-Day veterans had gathered by the Dakota. They could not contain their excitement, and we mingled together meeting them and talking about our trip.

An aroused contingent of the international press decended on the scene. The veterans were the big story for the day, and every sort of media hound was there for photos or video of the veterans as they went through a rehearsal on board the airplane with the young jumpmasters.

For most of the veterans, the vibrations and sounds and smells of the Dakota brought back the past in a rush of emotion.

During the practice session, the 26 veterans who would jump from our Dakota were animated, clowning and joking with one another while the press swarmed around them. But when the time came to load up, chutes on, a somber mood prevailed.

The jumpmasters had done their best to prepare the vets for the jump ahead. Sgt. Albert Dempsey, 34: Sgt. Carlos Sanchez, 35: and Capt. Dave Kanamine, 35 treated the veterans with respect while instructing them on the jump. When we were finally nearing the drop zone and the first stick of six vets stood to hook up, the younger members of the 82nd could not resist a few rousing shouts of "Airborne!"

I had the E-ticket. While Epps and Harless piloted the airplane, and Brooks and Hand sat up front, I was inches away from the open jump door. Sitting on a steel tool box along with Berndt Birkholz, the video cameraman, I was shooting still pictures with one hand and reaching over with the other to trip the shutter release for a remote camera I had mounted on the outside of the plane.

As each of the men moved to the door, they looked back over their shoulder toward the jumpmaster. I couldn't help feeling a swell of pride for what these guys were doing. They were young again, and the looks on their faces were cast from determination, laced with just a smidgen of fear. But they all went out the door.

During one pass over the DZ, Epps had cheated down on the altitude to stay clear of clouds. The jumpmasters waved off the next stick, so on the next circuit, Epps bore a hole through a couple of clouds to remain at 3400 feet AGL. The jumpers were going to jump, no matter what.

Suddenly, the plane seemed empty. We'd done it: the airborne was out the door. The jumpmasters gathered around the door, straining to see open chutes.

Epps circled the DZ a couple of times, lingering longer than the controllers below would have liked. He finally wheeled around toward Omaha Beach as 16 C-130s bore down on the DZ to drop a battalion of the 82nd and 101st Airborne.

The whole thing, of course, was immensely successful. Images of the veterans hurtling out of the Dakota were on every TV screen and newspaper around the world. But the limelight fell short of the Dakota. The story of how it had made it to France to complete its mission, in spite of the difficulties encountered, is known only to readers of this account.

Brooks liked it that way. He brought the airplane to France to honor the memory of his father, who was an airman during the war, and to honor the efforts of the veterans who had worked so hard to make the jump happen. The emotional current that ran through the airplane was thanks enough.

On the ground, the media circus surrounded the veterans and their jump. But in the Dakota, on the way to the DZ, those old guys were by themselves. In each face there was apitched look mixing pride with a little sadness. They had all done this 50 years ago, when the stakes were life or death. Most of their friends were lost, and it was for them that these men jumped again.

Mission accomplished. (By Todd H. Huvard)

~ ~ ~

FROM DOUGLAS TO D-DAY

Don Brooks "D-Day Dakota," serial number 12425, began life as a C-47A in January 1944 when it rolled off the assembly line in Oklahoma City. Assigned to the Royal Air Force as a Dakota III and given a new serial number KG395, the Dakota was ferried to Down Ampney in England and entered service with 48 Squadron, one of five squadrons of the 46 Group.

While based at Down Ampney, the Dakota and its crew practiced daily for the upcoming invasion of Europe. Dakotas would carry paratroopers, tow gliders and transport supplies and wounded soldiers.

Action for this particular Dakota came on the eve of D-Day, when it took off from Down Ampney towing a Horsa glider carrying reinforcements and headed for the beaches of Normandy. The Dakota returned to its base unscathed.

Following the initial invasion, the plane spent several months flying resupply and ferry missions in support of the advancing allied troops.

During operation Market-Garden, the Dakota flew numerous mission to Arnhem in the Netherlands as part of the campaign that was popularized by the book and the movie "A Bridge Too Far." During the operation, the plane was transferred to 437 Squadron, a Royal Canadian Air Force unit based at Blakehill Farm.

Its major campaign came in 1945 during Operation Varsity, the largest and final airborne offensive of the war in Europe. With its offensive duties completed, the Dakota was relegated to fly supply and ferry missions, transporting prisoners of war and refugees.

At the end of the war, the Dakota was flown back to Canada and remained in service with the Royal Canadian Air Force until 1970. Declared surplus, it was sold to Owen Wilson of Calgary, Canada, in 1973, and eventually resold to Energy, Inc. of Corpus Christi, Texas, in 1985. One year later, the airplane was bought by Basler Flight Service Inc., which in turn sold it to Flight Services, Inc. of Panama City, Fla.

The airplane now belongs to Don Brooks Aviation, Inc., of Douglas, Georgia which bought it in 1989, and then loaned to the Greenland Expedition Society, flown by Pat Epps, equipped with skis to recover a P-38 of the 'Lost Squadron' buried for fifty years under 264 feet of ice. The P-38 is being reassembled in a hanger in Middlesboro, Kentucky, to fly again.

D-DAY Remembered 1944

My Rendezvous With Destiny

It was just nine months after the surprise Japanese bombing of Pearl Harbor, and our country was in total mobilization for war against the Axis Powers.

I had taken a job at the Wright Aircraft Engine plant in Loveland, Ohio shortly after the war started to do my part like everyone else that was not already in the service. I was too young for the draft, and the company was getting deferrments for the employees.

It was after I saw that Army Poster, the one showing paratroopers dropping from the sky carrying Thompson Sub Machine Guns, that I knew what I wanted to do.

I enlisted at age nineteen on August 19,1942 as a volunteer for the parachute infantry at Fort Thomas, Kentucky. Ordered to report to a mountain training camp at Toccoa, Georgia, where I became an original member of the just forming 506 Parachute Infantry Regiment and the 101st Airborne Division, the Screaming Eagles. Our regiment was the first unit formed to take basic combat training on the mountain called Currahee. This word in Indian means 'Standing Alone,' and became our battle cry.

After three months of rigorous physical training in the mountains of north Georgia, we were ordered to Fort Benning. Our second battalion, 535 men, began the trip with a 120 mile forced march to Atlanta with full battle gear and temperatures below freezing at night. Thirty caliber machine guns and eighty-one millimeter mortars were passed from man to man to carry on their shoulders until they gave out. It took three days to complete the march. Mayor William B. Hartsfield of Atlanta met us at five corners where our forced march was hailed as a world record feat. *(Atlanta airport was named in his honor)*

Then on to Fort Benning by train where we received our silver wings after completing five parachute jumps in December of 1942.

I bunked near a guy that was a cartoonist, Joe Wittzerman, and below is a sample of how my letters to my mother looked.

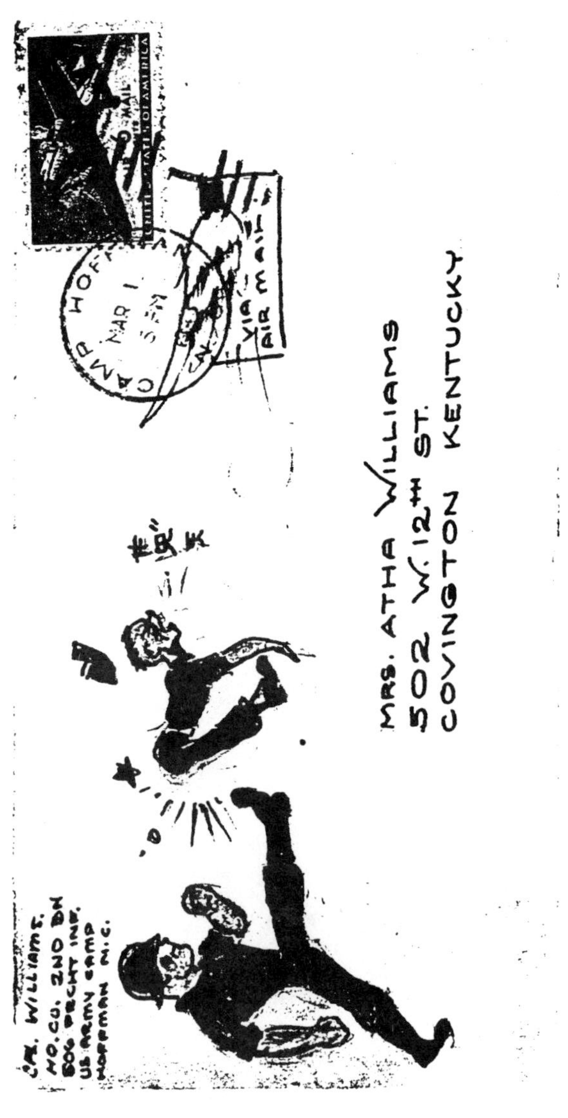

Photo supplied by The Associated Press Ltd.

The 101st Abn stands inspection for the Prime Minster of England, Sir Winston Churchill, accompanied by Generals Dwight D. Eisenhower, Omar N. Bradley, and Maxwell B. Taylor one month before D-Day, Southern England May 1944. All unit shoulder patches were removed at this time.

Moving on to Camp Mackall *(named in honor of the first paratrooper killed in Sicily)* and Fort Bragg, North Carolina.

After maneuvers in Tennessee, we shipped overseas from New York's Camp Shanks September 1943 on the British troop ship HMS Samaria, which later was sunk in the Mediterranean Sea.

Based near Swindon, England in the tiny village of Aldbourne, and living in a Nisson Hut, we continued to train for the forth coming allied invasion of Europe. I was subsequently promoted to Sergeant. On pass to Swindon, Joe Slosarczyk and I had our

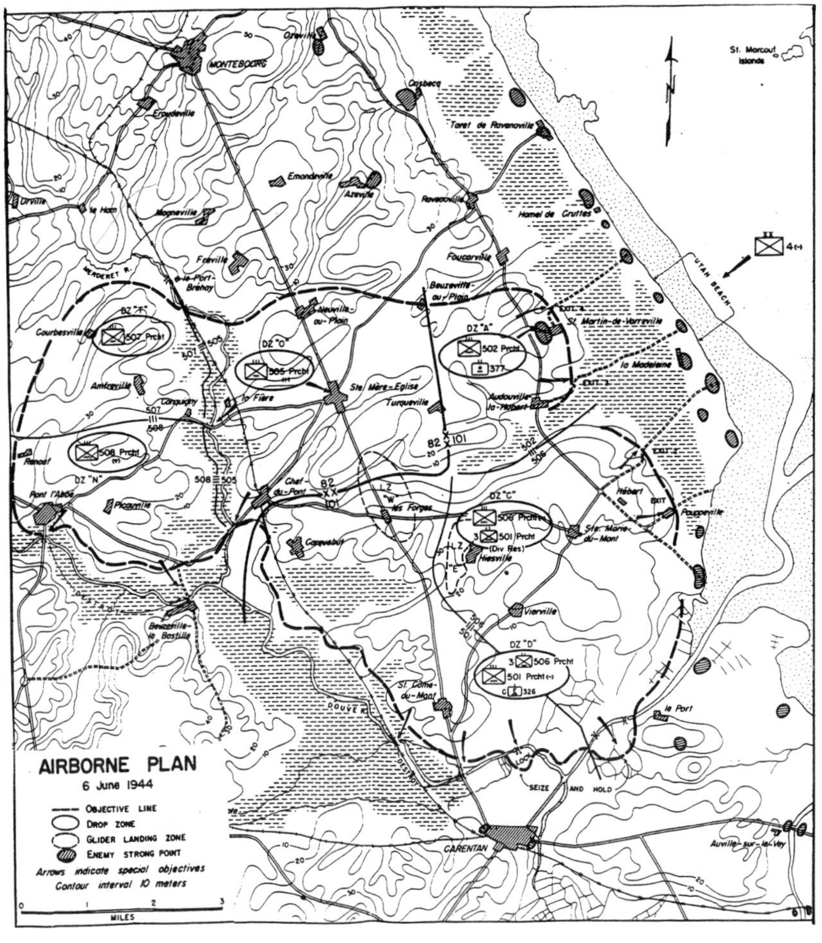
AIRBORNE PLAN
6 June 1944
OBJECTIVE LINE
DROP ZONE
GLIDER LANDING ZONE
ENEMY STRONG POINT
Arrows indicate special objectives
Contour interval 10 meters
MILES
MONTEBOURG
CARENTAN
UTAH BEACH
Ste Mère-Eglise
Chef-du-Pont
Pont l'Abbé
St. Marcouf Islands
DZ "T"
507 Prcht
DZ "O"
505 Prcht
DZ "A"
502 Prcht
377
DZ "N"
508 Prcht
DZ "C"
506 Prcht
501 Prcht
DZ "D"
326
SEIZE AND HOLD

picture taken together which later became a treasured possession. "For someone to remember me by," he said at the time.

It was while on a final practice parachute jump for the invasion, near the southern coast, that I was treated to a close look at the leaders of the free world. Generals Dwight D. Eisenhower, Maxwell B. Taylor, Omar N. Bradley, and the prime minister of England, Sir Winston Churchill. Their open command car stopped near me in a field in which we had just landed. They got out and watched as we took our positions.

About June 2, 1944, we moved into a marshaling area in southern England. On Monday afternoon June 5, General Taylor appeared among a small group of us. He reminded us of what the invasion meant to the future history of the world and free people every where. He said "I will be with you tonight in France, and I pray that God will be with every one of you. We have a *rendezvous with destiny*."

A worried General Ike likewise was milling among the paratroopers, and was heard to say, "Men, give me all you've got for three days and I will have you back in London with your girl friends by the end of the week." ...It was more like four weeks.

In line for our evening meal we were served steak and ice cream, it had never happened before. A symbolic last supper?

General Dwight D. Eisenhower, Allied Commander-In-Chief had given his orders of the day for June 6, which read-

"Soldiers, sailors, and airmen of the Allied Expeditionary Force!"

"You are about to embark on a great crusade. The eyes of the world are upon you and the hopes and prayers of all liberty loving people go with you."

"In company with our brave Allies and brothers in arms on other fronts you will bring about the destruction of the

German war machine, elimination of Nazi tyranny over the oppressed peoples of Europe and security for ourselves in a free world."

"Your task will not be an easy one. Your enemy is well trained, well equipped and battle hardened. He will fight savagely. But in this year of 1944 much has happened since the Nazi triumph of 1940 and 1941."

"The United Nations have inflicted upon the Germans great defeats in open battle, man to man."

"Our air offensive has seriously reduced their strength in the air and their capacity to wage war on the ground, our home fronts have given us overwhelming superiority in weapons and munitions of war and have placed at our disposal great reserves of trained fighting men."

"The tide has turned and free men of the world are marching together to victory."

"I have full confidence in your courage, devotion to duty and skill in battle. We will accept nothing less than full victory. Good luck and let us all beseech the blessings of Almighty God upon this great and noble undertaking."

~ ~ ~

In the remaining daylight, about 10:00 PM, we boarded C-47 troop carrier planes at Uppottery Airfield to take us across the English Channel to France. Underneath our plane, with the registration number 315046, and chalk number 48, the crew had attached four release brackets to carry containers of ammunition. With takeoff at 11:05 PM with the planes nine across, it formed a column 300 miles long. This assembly took two hours before the planes headed for France for our jump. It was very windy and many men got sick from the long bumpy ride in the dark.

On the evening of June 5, 1944, at Uppottery airfield, England, this message was read to all men of the 506th Parachute Infantry, just prior to take off aboard the C-47 troop carriers for the night drop into Normandy.

OFFICE OF THE REGIMENTAL COMMANDER

Soldiers of the Regiment: D-DAY

Today, and as you read this, you are enroute to that great adventure for which you have trained for over two years.

Tonight is the night of nights.

Tomorrow the whole of our homeland and the Allied world the bells will ring out tidings that you have arrived, and the invasion for liberation has begun.

The hopes and prayers of your near ones accompany you, the confidence of your high commanders goes with you. The fears of the Germans are about to become a reality.

Let us strike hard. When the going is tough, let us go harder. Imbued with faith in the rightness of our cause, and the power of our might, let us annihilate the enemy where found.

May God be with each of you fine soldiers. By your actions let us justify His faith in us.

(signed) R. Sink
Colonel

June 5, 1944

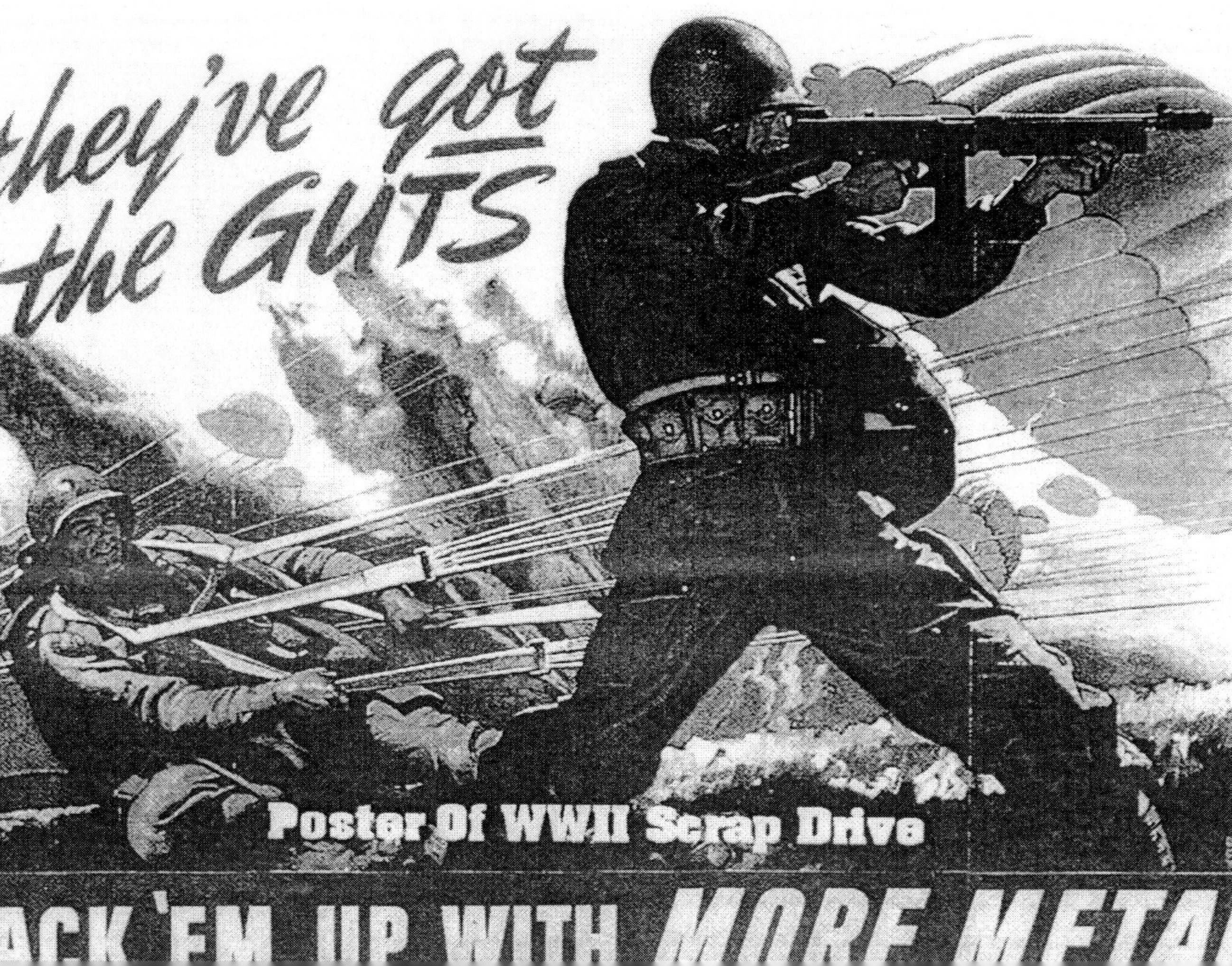

Poster Of WWII Scrap Drive

At this time for the historic record, I list the manifest of my plane in jump order, consisting of seventeen men. *(It took fifty years to find a copy list of these men as I could not remember one single name.)*

Lt. Colonel Robert L. Strayer, 0-314419

Lt. George Lavahsol, 0-1286510

Lt. Peter Baranowski, 0-1291059

Sgt Benjamin J. Stoney, KIA, 39530033

Sgt. Robert L. Williams, 15117139

Cpl. Harold R. Hendershot, 1262633

Sgt. Earl A. Hale, 39393613

Cpl. William Maslowski, 20543460

Jack O. Ginn, 39698879

Pvt. J. McCormick, 14083071

T4 Arthur R. Hartman, 13150694

PFC David B. Henderson, 29352233

PFC John J. Flanagan, 16001180

PFC Andrew R. Campbell, 14543457

PFC Harold E. Wygel, 15230650

PFC G. Kuntz, 39311311

CPL C. Bryant, 14124497

Plane crew of 315046, 92nd TC Squadron, 439th TC Group (2nd serial)

2nd Lt. Donald Q. Reid F.O.

2nd Lt. William F. Shotwell

Sgt. Arthur M. Hackett

Sgt. William C. Roker

(Pilot Reid and crew chief Hackett were killed when our plane crashed Nov. 19, 1944 near Brighton, England)

We crossed the French coast between the channel islands of Jersey and Gernsey receiving the first enemy anti-aircraft fire. The bursting shells shoved the plane one way, then another. Realizing the war had started, I sat staring at the open door opposite me, waiting for the order to stand up and hook up when a plane in full view, blew up with a terrific explosion. It had carried eighteen men of our third battalion, and three crew members of the 440th TC Group. A few moments later the green light came on. At 1:30 AM, June 6, D-Day we parachuted onto Nazi occupied French soil just a little north-east of Ste-Mere Eglise, near the tiny village of Foucarville, Normandy. Our pilot's strong evasive action and flying very low, estimated at six hundred fifty feet, resulted in our paratroops being widely scattered. The get ready light came on and everyone began to struggle to their feet with the heavy load every man carried. Every man hooked up and then hung on to the static line cable for dear life as the bombs bursting in the air made flying straight impossible. Mercifully, the green light came on, and the first four men in front of me disappeared into the moonlight.

Many, many times I have been asked what were my thoughts as I left that shaky airplane, and entered the dark unknown. Until now I have never answered truthfully, not wanting to admit how scared I was. I did not have to think about my movements, as they had been drilled into me for two years, and I acted automatically. At the moment I struggled out that open door I had only one thought, and I don't exactly know where it came from. In fact I remember so clearly I think I must have said it out loud,....*though I walk through the valley of the shadow of death, I shall fear no evil.* I was praying folks, I was preparing to die. For these many years, that has been a very personal thing with me.

I landed in water chest deep just seconds after my chute opened. Many of us learned for the first time that the Germans had marsh areas filled with sea water as they tried to eliminate possible landing areas. With a surprise landing I went completely under water three feet deep, and struggling to straighten up, realized it was going to be a job getting the wet harness off. Thank goodness the Mae West I was wearing did not activate, or I would have had to cut my way out. Within five minutes I saw a shadowy figure, then heard my first cricket click challenge, *click-clack.* My heart was in my mouth as I fumbled to find my cricket. I said 'wait' in a loud whisper, then he said 'Flash,' an alternative identification option. I quickly returned the counter sign, 'Thunder', and threw in a *click-clack* for good measure. Soon two more joined us, making four of us trying to decide which way to go to get out of the water. One man felt the hard surface of a road under his feet and we headed in what I believe was a northerly direction and shallow water. About twenty minutes passed before we moved out of the water onto dry ground. Suddendly out of the darkness ahead of us came a rapid burst of machine gun fire. We had met the enemy for the first time by walking in the dark straight toward a machine gun nest. Abruptly I was spun to my left, and then realized something had gone through my left pants leg pocket.

We knew we had run into Germans as they had orders to shoot, and we did not. Our orders were to use knives and grenades until daylight.

In the darkness, I let myself tumble into the water that was along side the road, attempting to feign death. As I crouched there with just my nose and mouth out of the water, I realized their bullets could not reach me. Then another machine gun started a traversing fire off in the distance to my left. I knew I was in their line of fire and they could see me if not for the darkness.

With day light just a few hours away, I knew I had to get out of there and began moving slowly back in the direction we came. At the same time I began to feel my leg to see how badly I was hit. To my amazement I found twelve holes in the large left hand trouser pocket of my jumpsuit, my D-Rations had blown out with everything else that was in there, but no blood. I could not believe

I was not hit. Two of the men had been killed in the middle of that road, and I have always believed that those bullets passed through one of them before going through my pocket. I had gone to the right, the fourth man had gone to the left side and disappeared into the water.

The farther I moved away from that encounter, the more I stood up, until the water was only a foot deep as it started to get light, with the sounds of battle heard in every direction, but not too close.

As the first rays of daylight penetrated the dark blue sky, I saw formations of B-26 bombers making their run west to east in line with the beach gun emplacements. As the clusters of bombs dropped, the sun was gleaming off the bottoms of the airplanes, and the ground explosions were chasing each other along the beach about two miles away. The small puffs of ack-ack began to fill the sky in front of the planes. One found it's mark and I watched as a bomber turned into a red ball of fire when it exploded. It was hard to believe what I was seeing when more of them got hit.

The weight of my wet clothes and equipment, a .45 caliber Sub Thompson, a pouch with six twenty round clips, gas mask, musette bag, canteen, pickshovel, long underwear, and four hand grenades became too much. Exhausted I laid across a big wild rose bush growing out of the water, ignoring the thorns. Some minutes later, and with full daylight coming on, I saw three men moving slowly toward me with their rifles pointed in my direction. Luckily they were our guys and they provided a couple of shoulders to lean on.

We could see a barn in the distance setting on higher ground with what we decided was a few of our men milling around. As we headed for it, we were pinned down momentarily by rifle fire somewhere off in the distance to our left, but I was tired of that water, and continued to head for the barn and dry ground. When my companions realized the sniper was a lousy shot, they followed my lead. We got to dry ground where about twenty others had gathered with three German prisoners, and an excited Frenchmen.

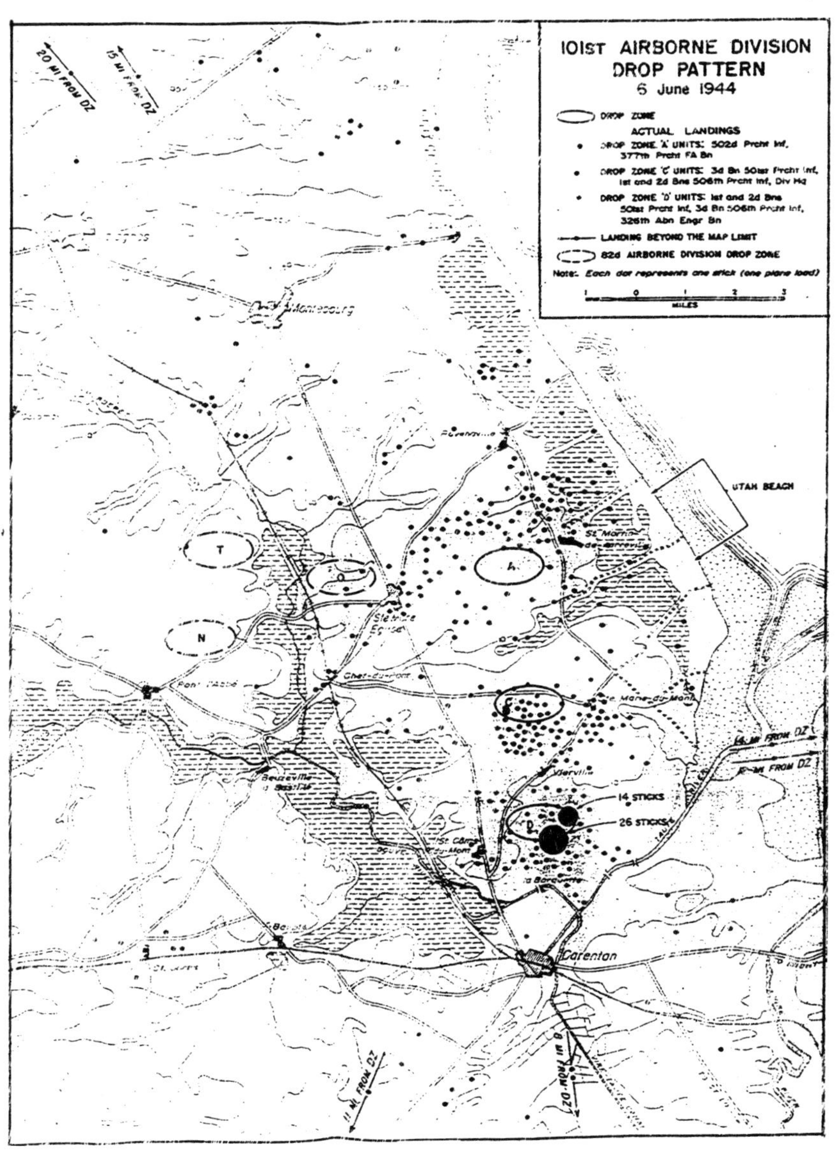
101st AIRBORNE DIVISION
DROP PATTERN
6 June 1944
DROP ZONE
ACTUAL LANDINGS
DROP ZONE 'A' UNITS: 502d Prcht Inf, 377th Prcht FA Bn
DROP ZONE 'C' UNITS: 3d Bn 501st Prcht Inf, 1st and 2d Bns 506th Prcht Inf, Div Hq
DROP ZONE 'D' UNITS: 1st and 2d Bns 501st Prcht Inf, 3d Bn 506th Prcht Inf, 326th Abn Engr Bn
LANDING BEYOND THE MAP LIMIT
82d AIRBORNE DIVISION DROP ZONE
Note: Each dot represents one stick (one plane load)
MILES
20 MI FROM DZ
15 MI FROM DZ
Montebourg
UTAH BEACH
Ste Mère Eglise
Pont l'Abbé
Chef-du-Pont
Vierville
14 STICKS
26 STICKS
Carentan
11 MI FROM DZ
8 MI FROM DZ
FROM DZ
T
N
O
A
C
D

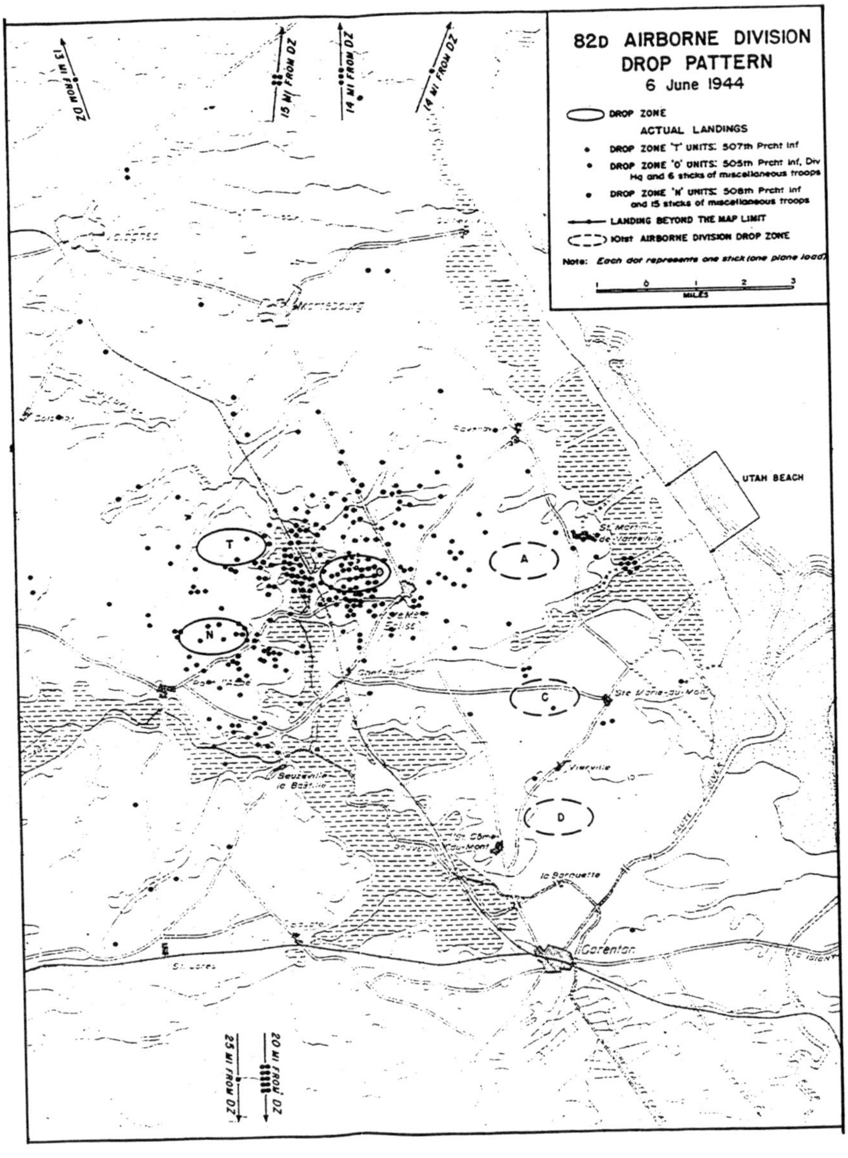
82D AIRBORNE DIVISION
DROP PATTERN
6 June 1944
DROP ZONE
ACTUAL LANDINGS
DROP ZONE 'T' UNITS: 507th Prcht Inf
DROP ZONE 'O' UNITS: 505th Prcht Inf, Div Hq and 6 sticks of miscellaneous troops
DROP ZONE 'N' UNITS: 508th Prcht Inf and 15 sticks of miscellaneous troops
LANDING BEYOND THE MAP LIMIT
101st AIRBORNE DIVISION DROP ZONE
Note: Each dot represents one stick (one plane load)
MILES
13 MI FROM DZ
15 MI FROM DZ
14 MI FROM DZ
14 MI FROM DZ
UTAH BEACH
T
O
N
A
C
D
Carentan
Ste Marie-du-Mont
Vierville
Beuzeville la Bastille
la Barquette
20 MI FROM DZ
25 MI FROM DZ

After discovering we had landed near Foucarville, two miles from the Channel and Utah Beach, two and a half miles north of our intended drop zone, we formed a staggered column and moved out to the south toward Ste Marie-Du-Mont, more or less following route D-14 through Audoville. Gathering mostly 101st, a few 82nd troopers as we went, only engaging Germans when we had to. Trying to avoid them when we could, to get on to the place we were supposed to be, and take our objectives. Slowly the units began to take shape.

On the morning of June 7, we caught up with a group that consisted mostly of my own headquarters company, and for the first time I was with my very close buddies, a good feeling. Gradually our Second Battalion, under Lt. Col. Robert L. Strayer, was becoming a fighting force. Exits 1 and 2 from Utah Beach, two of our objectives had been taken on June sixth allowing units of the 4th Division armor to begin pouring inland, and we moved to the southwest.

Mid-morning we moved toward the village of Vierville and since our First Battalion had passed through early that morning with hardly a shot fired, we were surprised when we were ambushed in the center of town. The Germans had a machine gun in a church tower, and a line of infantry entrenched parallel to the road. Sergeant Benjamin J. Stoney *(Native American)* took a burst of machine gun fire in the face as he peered around a stone wall to return fire, and was killed. He had jumped just ahead of me from plane number 48. He was fourth, I was fifth. The battle lasted most of the afternoon around his body. As we fought them off, we began to run low on ammunition.

We became even more concerned when the sound of a tank could be heard approaching. Everyone looked in that direction as it rounded a bend and seemed to stare at us. It seemed to be as afraid of us as we were of it. After looking down its gun barrel a few minutes we realized it was one of ours, a welcome sight, and the first tank we saw from the Utah beach landing. When we all pointed to the church tower the big gun raised, and with one shot from the 105 canon blew a big hole in the tower dropping the Germans and their guns down on the lobby below. We learned our enemy was a reinforced company of the German 6th Parachute Regiment.

Our platoon leader, Lt. Baranowski, climbed on top of the tank and got the crew to mount the big .50 Caliber machine gun on top. He manned that gun like a mad man, *(we called him the mad Russian, he later was badly wounded in Holland)*, killing Germans left and right as fast as he could shoot.

When the enemy began to wave white flags wanting to surrender, the firing slacked off, except for the gun on the tank. Major Horton had to draw his Colt .45, and point it at the Lt. to make him stop shooting. In a short time we captured more Germans then we knew what to do with. One hundred twenty-five prisoners, one hundred-twenty five dead. We had six wounded, one dead.

Our regimental commander, Colonel Sink, arrived by jeep and ordered our unit southwest down the road toward Beaumont to help the First Battalion, which was held up by the enemy. He had just witnessed the death of his friend, and the First Battalion's commander, Colonel Turner. Turner had climbed on top a tank to direct fire when shot through the head by a sniper bullet just as he had turned to look back at Colonel Sink.

After five days and a complete assembly of our battalion, we arrived at the small village of Les Droueries on a hill over looking the city of Carentan. In the small orchard beside the road, there were many dead Germans in and around a mortar pit that our mortars had knocked out before our advance. Scouting a nearby woods I found a dead GI with an apparent booby trap grenade under him. I saw a teen age French girl approaching, looking around, possibly for food. I warned her away as I gave her a bar of chocolate D-Ration. The war left my mind momentarily.

Before us was a large marshy area with two causeways leading to Carentan, about a mile away. Biding our time while tank guns to our rear shelled the city with airburst for a day. Resting in a small German dug foxhole, I was startled to see a lone ME-109 at tree top level. It was quick, but I swear I saw the pilot wave.

A lone enemy plane came over that evening with bombs trying to get the tank guns behind me that were shelling Carentan. The next day plans were made to infiltrate around to the outskirts of Carentan after dark.

It took all night sneaking quietly, but quickly, across one of the causeways, past 'dead man's corner' and up a small ravine before arriving at daylight at the last house on the edge of town. Not a shot had been fired.

Hell started all over again as the Germans realized we where there. Slowly we spread out to the west meeting heavy resistance in the afternoon. We were pinned down and almost surrounded. Leaning against a three foot embankment with a hedge on top, better known as a hedge row, I was peering through binoculars I had taken from the body of a German officer to spot something or somebody to shoot at. The enemy must have thought I was an artillery spotter and quickly got off two shots with eighty-eight millimeter artillery with flat projectory straight at me. One shell hit the other side of the bank in front of me, the other came over the top and hit the bank in back of me on the other side of the road. *(Later I was told there was four shells)* Besides the ear shattering noise, plus concussion, the air was filled with dust and dirt. I was not hit, but as soon as I could see, I threw the binoculars down and started to moved away from that spot. Stumbling out of the cloud of dust, a friend saw me and exclaimed, "Willie! Your alive, man how did you get through that? I thought you were dead for sure!".

It was here on June 13 that my good buddy, Joseph Slosarczyk, one of my radio men, took a bullet through the chest. He had been told to stay with D company, as they needed a radio badly during hard fighting. He had begged Sgt. Falvey for relief, complaining as we all were of exhaustion. Falvey had no one else to send but Joe, and Joe went. Disturbed by guilt after Joe was killed, Falvey later transferred to a bazooka *(anti-tank)* team, where he would not have to give orders for a mission that did not also include him. Dick Falvey, ... Irish, tough, brave, emotional and tender hearted.

Joe had predicted many times that he would die in combat, and it only took eight days to prove his intuition right. Known to men in our platoon as Joking Joe, he is buried in the beautiful American cemetery at Colleville-St-Laurent near Pointe du Hoc. *(Omaha Beach)*

Captain Gross, commander of D company, was killed not far from Joe. My company commander, Captain Cox, was badly wounded, evacuated to England, recovered and returned to duty. Our enemy here was S.S. Panzer Grenadiers, and German parachute troops of the 6th Prcht. Regt. with four Mark IV tanks.

What followed was probably the worst night our unit experienced in the war, due to our losses, the exhaustion, and the expectation of being over-run by the enemy. At daylight we resumed the attack until relieved by 2nd Bn 502.

On June 14, as we headed back toward Carentan, we passed a building the Germans had used as a hospital. Our medics were moving into it caring for Germans and Americans. I must have looked extremely dirty, and beat as a medic pulled me inside and said Sgt., 'I am going to give you something to let you sleep awhile.' I just made it to a second story back bedroom couch before I slumped into a very deep sleep. When I awoke the following morning the entire back wall of the building was gone, and I was looking down into the back yard. Some time during the night, an artillery shell had hit the back wall of the little hospital.

On D-Day plus nine, Thursday, June 15, we had won our objective and had moved back into Carentan for a few days rest while an occasional enemy eighty-eight shell hit somewhere in the city.

Our division was re-equipped and returned to the bases in England, while our army turned north to capture the strategic port of Cherburg. It took almost three months for the Allies to complete the battle for the Cotentin Peninsula, before the drive for Paris.

I firmly believe that 'our first duty is to remember' the fallen and forgotten men of D-Day, like my friend Joe Slosarczyk, who gave all. This was my intention as I returned to Normandy by parachute, on the fiftieth anniversary of D-Day to honor those men on June 6, 1994. The picture of Joe Slosarczyk was in my left breast pocket when I jumped................ He is remembered.

Robert L. Williams ASN 15117139

August 19, 1942_December 1, 1945

Highest Rank, Sergeant

DOB September 28,1922

POB Covington, Kentucky USA

Life member__101st Airborne Association

__Veterans of Foreign Wars

The information in this entire book is on record in the Eisenhower Center, D-Day Museum, New Orleans, Louisiana. Dr. Stephen E. Ambrose, Director.

LIST OF EQUIPMENT I CARRIED ON NORMANDY JUMP

D-Day June 6, 1944 (*Plus a T-5 parachute approximately 40 pounds.)*

Personal
Drawers, wool.
Undershirt, wool.
Socks, wool.
Jump Jacket, gas impregnated, insignia.
Jump Pants.
Helmet, complete and camo net.
Trousers, OD.
Shirt, OD.
Boots, dubbing
Suspenders.
Belt, web waist.
Handkerchief, 2.
Dogtags, & chain.
Wallet
Trench knife, M3.
Thompson .45 M1A1.
Pouch, 6-20rd clips.
Hand grenades, 2-Mk2 A1

Medical Equipment
Sulfanilimide powder.
Shell dressings, 2.
Insecticide.
1 roll tape.
Sulphadiazine tablets.
First Aid packet, parachute.
Halazone tablets.
3 rubbers.
Cupric sulphate sponge.

Individual Basic
Field bag, M1936.
Dispatchcase, M1938.
Suspenders.
First Aid pouch.
Spoon.
Canteen & cover.
Cartridge belt.
Carrying strap.
First Aid packet.
Canteen cup.

In Field Bag
Raincoat.
Toilet articles.
Wool socks, 3 pr.
Bath towel.
Handkerchiefs, 2.
50 sheets toilet paper

Chemical Warfare
Gas mask.
Eyeshields, 2.
Sleeve detector.
Cape.
Protective ointment.
Reference card.
Eye ointment.
Shoe impregnate.

(Not listed: Rations, cigarettes.)

~Joking Joe Jones~

Arriving at Toccoa, Georgia, on a hot August day in 1942, at age nineteen, I found myself with a group of young men from all parts of the United States, with backgrounds derived from all kinds of nationalities. A mongrel group if there ever was one. All civilians except for the cadre, *(leaders)* volunteering for special US Army training to become the first Parachute Regiment to start from basic training, the now famous 506. Many had last names that gave the mail orderly fits at mail call resulting in delay and temper from guys impatient to get mail from home. It meant you were in for some kidding, and probably a new nickname as this truly American group came together and began combat training for the deadly task of invading Hitler's Europe. Being from Kentucky, I got hit with "Hill-a-gin," but later they just called me "Willie," short for Williams. Nicknames seemed to come from comic strips, *(a common denominator)* and necessary for the guys with long, hard to pronounce, last names. Bubble Nose, Sleepy, Dude, Piggy, etc.

Joseph Slosarczyk, from Wisconsin's Polish community, was one of those young men. Joe was a likable lummox type and a healthy specimen. He was about nineteen, blond, very solid, with a big chest, which like his arms and legs, was devoid of hair. He became "Hairless Joe."

He was even tempered and easily took the extra tough training program that seemed to keep us busy night and day. In the following months, Joe acquired more nicknames. He would attempt to trade snide remarks with the sharpies of the platoon, and the result was, "Slow Joe," that I thought was a little cruel. Another came from the clumsy way he related a joke. He always loused it up, but the guys enjoyed this more than the joke because he was so funny. So more often, and with affection, he was known as "Joking Joe Jones" or "Joking Joe."

Because of his slowness, Joe got his promotions slowly and only because our platoon officer was a 'Mad Russian' *(Baranowski)* and could relate to Joe's Polish background. He did get to Private First Class, while I went on to Buck Sergeant, and one of his leaders in the communications platoon. When told to do something, Joe might grumble a little, following the example of the other men, but there was no question in his mind he would try to do the task. The trouble was, he always seemed to be in the wrong place at the wrong time.

I liked Joe, everybody did. Even the Officers couldn't get mad at him when he did something ridicules. Like the time we marched out to a clearing in the pine trees where a young hotshot officer from West Point was about to instruct us in the art of unarmed combat. Looking around the group of "green" recruits, his gaze stopped at Joe. The Louie thought Joe looked easy. "Come here soldier and let me demonstrate how to break the leg scissors hold!" Joe went over to where the officer had placed himself on the ground and dutifully got a scissors grip across his middle. "Now I don't want you to be easy on me, I want you to hunker down when I tell you," the officer instructed him. Looking around at the rest of us to be sure we didn't miss his expertise, he said "Now". Joe's legs stiffened and before the officer could apply his counter action, his face got red, and he couldn't breathe, he couldn't do anything but gasp. It seemed as if it took Joe a long time to decide that things didn't go as they were supposed to... God, that was funny!

All of us except, the Louie, knew that Joe was a wrestler in high school, and all of us, except the Louie knew that Joe would do just what he was told to do. Everybody turned away to laugh while Joe got chewed out royally. Joe just stood there with a quizzical look on his face, while the officer tried to fight off a smile as he turned his back to us.

Eventually we finished parachute training, went on maneuvers and finally shipped out to England. Everybody was encouraged to send a picture to the folks back home before we went into combat. Joe could always get an argument by saying he knew he wasn't coming back, and he refused to bother about a picture. We would poke fun at him and try to explain nobody could predict the future, but he was adamant and never gave in on that point. His intuition became a boring subject to the rest of us.

It was during training maneuvers in North Carolina that I had to deliver sad telegrams to Joe, on two different occasions, which resulted in emergency leave for him. If memory serves me right, one was about his mother and the other his sister. Two deaths in just a few months caused me to believe he didn't have much family left. His older brother was in the Marines in the South Pacific. I had to wonder, did this have something to do with his belief that he wasn't coming back from the War?

One weekend before the invasion, Joe and I somehow got together on a pass to the English town of Swindon. Looking for something to do, I decided I should have a picture taken to send back home. Swindon was not a big town but it did have a commercial photographer. I asked Joe to join me in the studio, and he did. We had a picture made with Joe and me standing together. His comment was, "Somebody would have a picture to remember him by." I knew what he was saying but I didn't want to reply to that same old dumb stuff, so I let it go. That picture is still in my scrapbook fifty years later. Joe's copy never got home to his family, which I believe only consisted of a brother and sister.

Since Joe was not too swift with Morse code, and the Army had decided to add pigeons to our means of communication, he was chosen to be in charge of trying different ways of releasing them in the field during maneuvers. Soft hearted Joe got to love those birds and nobody dared to mistreat them. He would release them from our jump planes tucked in a paper sack to protect their feathers from the wind. They would escape the sack and fly back to our base. Although successful, most of the time they were released from the ground after our jump.

"D-DAY" finally came, and around 10 PM on June the 5th, we loaded on C-47's for the jump after midnight into occupied France. We were all loaded down with equipment, guns and ammunition, but Joe was also carrying two of his birds in paper sacks in a canvas bag hung below his reserve chute on his belly. He was confident that "His birds" would save the whole outfit by flying back to England with important information, and they could have. Others did.

The Germans, anticipating an invasion, had flooded many low lying fields and marsh areas with sea water. My fate was to land in one of these areas, and was relieved to find the water was only up to my chest. Still, it was a struggle to get out of the wet parachute harness in the dark loaded down with equipment, and aware of a shadowy figure just yards away, sounding like a cricket, waiting for a counter sign.

Come daylight, I learned that Joe landed in deeper water and he almost drowned as others did that night *(At least 36).* After making his way out of the water at daylight, Joe discovered that his beloved pigeons had drowned. It was a tragedy to Joe. Heart breaking, yet funny to the rest of us as we remembered the many months of serious training he had put in. To the credit of those tough but compassionate men, nobody laughed in front of Joking Joe Jones.

As we fought our way inland we used Joe as a radio operator. After about seven days *(I lost track of time)* our outfit infiltrated the German lines around Carentan at night. At daylight they fought back hard and the battle went on all day. Joe had manned a radio all night and day without relief with "D" Company, under enemy fire and about to be cut off. He pleaded with Sgt. Falvey for a relief radio man. He protested that he was exhausted and needed a break. When informed that he was the only man available for the job, he headed back to "D" Company. Joe believed in God and Country, he could not shirk his duty.

On the eight day, without hot food and little sleep on hard ground, we were engaged in the hottest combat yet. We were all scared, edgy, hungry and exhausted.

It was June 13, just several miles north of Carentan, in the orchards and hedge rows, about 4:OO P.M. that Joking Joe Jones, working the radio with "D" Company, for some reason stood up and caught a rifle bullet in the chest. It took just eight days in battle for Joe's prediction to come true. Just as he always said, he wasn't going home. Joe lies in the beautiful American cemetery at Colleville, France, with over 9,000 other Americans. *(Omaha Beach)*

While we had many wounded, Joe was the only one in my platoon to get killed in action. After fifty years, five or six of us get together for a few days every year at a reunion. We talk about Joking Joe Jones' intuition. A good soldier, an American hero that made a powerful contribution with courage and valor for his country.

It was for men like Joe that I returned to Normandy in June 1994, and, after fifty years again parachuted onto French soil, free French soil lest anyone has forgotten, to honor their memory and to let their families know they are with us in spirit. Also with me on that jump were two men that were in the same squad with Joe and I from the beginning of the 506th that hot August of 1942, fifty-four years ago. They are Richard Falvey and Gordon King. Thirty-eight other WW2 paratroopers participated. And yes, the picture of Joe was in my left breast pocket.

Joe's family was never told what happened to him or where he was buried, he was sort of missing in action. His brother Vitilas, who lives in Wisconsin, saw a picture of me holding Joe's picture beside his grave. He got my address from Gordon King, my Army buddy from Merrill, Wisconsin, and requested a copy of that picture. It seems they did not have many pictures of Joe, and none at all after he joined the Army. I decided to send the real McCoy, the one I had jumped with on the anniversary jump. It was not long before I got the picture back with a letter from Vitilas explaining that he had copies made and thought I should be the one to keep the original picture since I had been close to Joe when he died.

Vitilas has a son, Roger, that very much wanted to know something about his Uncle Joe. He called at Christmas, and we talked a long time. He has invited me to visit, I will certainly try...................Bob Williams.

ABOUT THE AUTHOR

Robert Leslie Williams

It is not difficult for one to understand where Mr. Williams patriotism comes from, by tracing his ancestors for several hundred years. Both sides of his family were represented in the American Revolutionary War and our fight for independence in 1776. His great, great, great, great grandfathers were among the young Americans of English decent that fought and accepted military land grants in the newly opened frontier after 1780.

After crossing the rugged Appalachian Mountains, John Williams and his family found their land along the upper Licking River near a place called Blue Licks (State Park), Nicholas County, Kentucky. It was also the sight of the last battle of the Revolutionary War.

On his mother's side, Frances Taylor arrived in this country from England in the early 1700's. His son Frances, and grandson Frances Jr., also accepted land grants for military service, and they too crossed the mountains to settle along the Kentucky River in Madison County, later along Eagle Creek, in Owen County.

During the American Civil War it was not uncommon to find his ancestors fighting in both the Union and Confederate Armies.

For two hundred years most all of them farmed, or had related occupations, blacksmiths, saddlers, etc., until Mr. Williams father Wm. H. took a job on the railroad and moved to Covington, Kentucky in the early 1900's.

There he met and married Miss Atha Taylor, whose father John, also had left the farm to become a Covington merchant.

Mr. Robert L. Williams, the fifth child was born near Fifteenth and Madison Avenue, Covington in 1922.

It was not long after leaving military service in 1945 that he returned to the country with his family to live, while employed in jewelry manufacturing, raised a herd of beef cattle, and eventually retire there.

Louis Washington

Profile

Gordon E. (Wren)King
101st Airborn Div., 506th Parachute Infantry Reg.
WW2 combat jumps in Normandy and Holland.
Communications-Radio operator
Born: June 4, 1924 in Omro, Wisconsin Age 69 (1994)
Address: Merrill, Wisconsin

Gordon enlisted at the age of 18 in the Paratroops in August 1942. He claims he never missed a Camp Toccoa hike, a training jump or a meal. He made all campaigns of Hq Co, except for two weeks in hospitals. He was the 2nd battalion radio operator in the regimental net, carrying an SCR 300 backpack radio behind Captain Charlie Shettle, the battalion executive officer and Major Oliver Horton. Captain Shettle was promoted to Colonel for his actions at the Douve locks on and after D-Day in Normandy. Major Horton was killed at Opeheusden in Holland.

Gordon spent three more years in the post WW2 period in the 82nd Airborne most of it in a pathfinder platoon. He took up skydiving from 1962 to 1968 and became USPA C level free-fall qualified with about 200 jumps.

He worked for 34 years for a Wisconsin Power Co., which he considers as tough, but satisifying, on utility lines at times forty feet in the air in thirty knot winds and the thermometer at 25 below. Gordon and his wife Margaret (Peg) had three daughters and have three grandchildren.

Profile

Richard (Red)Falvey
101st Airborne Div., 506th Parachute Infantry Reg.
WW2 combat jump in Normandy
Communications: Radio Operator and maintainer
Born: August 2, 1921 in Yonkers, NY., age 70 (1994)
Address: Hammondsport, NY

Richard joined the Army in August 1942. He volunteered for the paratroops, took his basic training at Taccoa, GA. and completed Ft. Benning parachute school on Dec. 25, 1942. He was assigned to the 101st AB Div.2nd Btn, Hqs Co. communication platoon. He jumped into Normandy about 1:15AM, June 6th, 1944 and landed near Foucarville. He joined a newly formed bazooka platoon for the Sept. 17th, 1944 parachute drop into Holland. He was wounded in Bastogne, Belgium, treated at an aid station, then sent back on line.

He returned to the U.S. with Hitler's and Goering's autos that were "captured" at Berchesgaden, Austria, and under auspices of the government toured the US after the war.

Richard married Leona in 1948 and had three children. He was employed as a brakeman and conductor by New York Central Railroad and retired in 1982 to Hammondsport, NY.

(Richard was on the Russian jump plane with Rollie Duff.)

Profile

Robert (Bob) Dunning
101st Airborne Div., 506th Parachute Infantry Reg.
WW2 combat jumps in Normandy & Holland
Rifleman
Born: September 3, 1921. Age. 72 (1994)
Address: Hartwell, GA

Robert completed Army basic training at Ft. McCellan, Alabama in 1942. After volunteering for the paratroops, he completed parachute school at Ft. Benning, GA. in 1943. He was assigned to the 101st AB Division, 506th PIR, Hq CO., 3rd. Btn. In Normandy all of the first stick of jumpers in his aircraft were either killed or captured. Bob was wounded in Holland in Operation Market Garden and was evacuted to England. He rejoined the 101st just in time to spend the middle of the winter in Bastogne surrounded by several German divisions.

Bob went to a one room country school until 6th grade. He excelled in track, football, boxing and became an Eagle Scout with 41 merit badges. His parents were farmers and he had one sister. His grandfather served with General Sherman during the Civil War. He graduated from the University of Georgia in 1951 with a BS and then in 1954 received a masters in education. During his professional career he served as a teacher, coach and school principal. He and his wife Myra have one son.

Profile

Troy Decker
101st Airborne Div., 506th Parachute Infantry Reg.
WW2 combat jumps in Normandy & Holland
Communication Sergeant
Born: April 15, 1922. Age 71 (1994)
Address: Connelly Springs, NC

Troy was born in Burke County, North Carolina in a log cabin and entered the army in April 1942. He completed parachute school in January 1943 following which he served with the 101st AB Division as communication sergeant from Toccoa, GA. to Berchesgaden, Austria. He was awarded the purple heart for wounds received in action.

Troy was discharged in September 1945 and subsequently started his own mechanical contracting business. After 30 years he retired in good health. He and his wife Margaret still live in North Carolina and they have four beautiful daughters. They celebrated their 50th wedding anniversary in June 1992.

Profile

Carl Beck
501st Parachute Infantry Reg.
WWII combat jumps in Normandy & Holland
Light mortar crewman
Born: November 21, 1925 Age 68 (1994)
Address: Atlanta, GA

Carl joined the army at 17 and volunteered for the airborne. He was asigned to the 501st PIR at Camp Toccoa, GA. After jump school at Ft. Benning and further training he deployed to England with the regiment and later took part in the Normandy, Holland, Bastogne and central European campaigns. He was wounded in Bastogne. He re-enlisted in the 82nd Airborne Division, was injured in a training jump but re-enlisted and retired as a master sergeant.

Carl retired after 28 years as a transportation engineer for Atlanta, GA. and now works part time for Agnes Scott College in Decatur, GA. He was widowed in 1993.

Profile

Richard Case
101st Airborne Division, 502nd ACRT
WWII combat jumps in Normandy & Holland
Demolition Specialist
Born: November 17, 1920 Age 73 (1994)
Address: Las Vegas, NV

Richard was activated in June 1943 from college into the Enlisted Reserve Corp. After basic training he volunteered for jump school and then demolition school. In the winter of 1943, after field training at Camp MacKall, NC. he was shipped as a replacement to the 502nd PIR near Hungerford, England. He jumped into Normandy the night of June 5th, 1944. After Normandy, he jumped into Holland in September 1944 and in mid-December went with the 101st Airborne Division into Bastogne, Belguim.

Richard was wounded twice. After discharge, he went to the University of California at Berkeley and graduated in 1948 with a Political Science degree. In 1950, he went back on active duty with the airborne serving with the 11th, 82nd and 101st divisions in Korea, retiring in 1962.

Presently, Richard and his wife for the past 20 years have owned a travel agency in Las Vegas.

Profile

Warren Wilt
82nd Airborne Div., 508th Parachute Infantry Reg.
WW2 combat Jump in Normandy
Radio operator and combat infantryman
Born: November 5, 1922 Age 71 (1994)
Abbeyville, KS

Warren volunteered for the airborne from the Military Police in Las Vegas and went through Ft. Benning Parachute School in July 1943 with the 541st. He was sent to England in 1944 where he was assigned to the 508th PIR and then jumped into Normandy on June 6th, 1944. He was involved in heavy fighting around St. Mere Eglise, was injured on June 26 and sent to England to recuperate. He joined the 508th in December 1944 for the Battle of the Bulge. In January 1945 he was sent to a hospital with frost bitten feet. Following the war he rejoined the Military Police and was assigned as a guard at President Trumans residence during the Potsdam conference. On December 24, 1945 he was discharged.

Warren is married, has two sons, two daughters and five grandchildren. He was employed for 32 years as an optician and has operated an Agriculture Service Center since 1978. He has taught diesel engines at Hutchinson Jr. College.

Profile

George Yochum
101st Airborne Div., 506th Parachute Infantry Reg.
WW2 combat jumps in Normandy & Holland
Messenger Dispatcher/Rifleman
Born: May 27, 1922 Age 72 (1994)
Address: San Diego, CA

George attended schools as a youth in Philadelphia, PA and entered the army from there in September 1942. He volunteered for the Airborne and participated with the 101st Airborne Division as a paratrooper in the invasions of Normandy & Holland and Battle of the Bulge and Rhineland campaigns.

On September 17th, 1944, George parachuted into Holland with the initial assault forces to secure the highway north to Arnhem so our trucks and infantry could cut the German forces in half. After 72 days of combat in Holland we had a short rest in France and were hauled by truck to stop the Germans break through in the Ardennes region (Battle of the Bulge area). Then on into Southern France and Berchesgaden, Austria and the end of the war.

After the war, George trained at the Philadelphia Museum College of Art and then in 1950 went weith TV Networks as a costume designer for 26 years until 1976. While with the Mike Douglas show, he entered politics as a councilman in New Jersey. He was elected for 3 terms and was council president for one term.

In show business he had the honor to make up Eisenhower when he appeared for a political event. "They tell me you were in the 101st," Ike said. "Yes sir," Yochum replied. "Who'd ever have thought an old soldier would come to this," Ike chuckled, as Yochum reached for a brush.

Profile

Robert (Bob) L. Williams
101st Airborne Div., 506th Parachute Infantry Reg.
WW2 combat jump in Normandy
Sergeant Communications Specialist
Born: September 28, 1922 in Covington, KY Age 71 (1994)
Union, KY

Bob volunteered for the paratroops at Ft. Thomas, KY on August 19, 1942. He was sent to Toccoa, GA where he became an original member of the 506th PIR of the 101st AB Division. The 506 was the first unit to take basic training on Curahee mountain. The word "Curahee" is an Indian name meaning standing alone. The 506th went through Parachute School at Ft. Benning, GA as a unit and graduated in December 1942. After training at Camp MacKall and Ft. Bragg they shipped overseas in September 1943 on the HMS Samaria and located near Swindon, England. On the evening of June 5, 1944 about 10:00PM they all boarded C-47 troop carrier aircraft and at l:15AM on June 6, parachuted into Normandy.

Eventually returning to England, Bob witnessed the terrible bombing of London by the German V2 rockets. He returned to New York on the Frederick Victory in December 1945, was discharged at Ft. Knox, KY and was home by Christmas.

Bob, a retired Diamond Setter, has two boys and one girl by his first marriage. The oldest son, a Vietnam veteran, was killed when his Cessna 208 crashed in September 1985 while carrying sixteen skydivers and a pilot. He was the subject of a book Bob wrote, called Cowboy's Caravan, ISBN No. 0-9627534-0-8. Bob is a life member of 101st Airborne Association and the VFW. He and his second wife, Barb, live in Union, KY and attend all the airborne reunions together.

Profile

Guy Whidden
101st Airborne Div., 502nd Parachute Infantry Reg.
WW2 combat jumps in Normandy & Holland
Rifleman, Parachute Training Instructor
Born: June 10, 1923 Age 70 (1994)
Frederick, MD

Guy was born and raised near Wyncote, PA. He enlisted shortly after Pearl Harbor, volunteered for the Airborne, completed Parachute School at Ft. Benning, GA and was then assigned to the 101st AB Division, 502nd PIR , 2nd Battalion of Hqs Company.

He made both Division combat jumps in Normandy and Holland. His saddiest and most traumatic experience was when a mortar round wounded himself and another man and killed two of his best friends. Compassion by an enemy perserved his life as he relates how he was struck from behind and pinned to the ground by a hulking German who put his Luger to his head. Probably a veteran of WW1 as he appeared old enough to be his father. Perhaps Guys youth reminded the German of a son of his own, as it seemed an eternity as Guy waited for the end. Suddenly, the German reversed the pistol, handed it to Guy, and surrendered much to his joy and relief.

Guy was wounded twice and returned to the states for hospital care and rehabilitation. He then was assigned as an "A" stage instructor in the Parachute School at Ft. Benning, GA until his discharge on November 7, 1945.

In 1950 Guy graduated from Salisbury State Teachers College in Maryland and then began a teaching career. He retired in 1979.

Profile ★

Arnold (Dutch) Nagel
82nd Airborne Div., 505th Parachute Infantry Reg.
WW2 combat jumps in Sicily, Salerno, Normandy and Holland
Staff Sergeant-Rifleman
Born: November 29, 1921, age 72 (1994) **Died**: August 15, 2000[1]
Address: Delphos, Ohio

Dutch came from a family of nine children. Their father died when he was nine years old. Dutch left home after the 8th grade and worked on a farm until going into the service. He joined the paratroops and after basic training at Macon, Georgia went to Parachute School at Fort Benning, Georgia. He was assigned to the 82nd AD Div., 505th PIR, C Company at Ft. Bragg, North Carolina. They left the states and arrived in Casablanca May 8, 1943. They jumped in Sicily and landed 65 miles from the drop zone. They then jumped in Salerno Bay and went through Naples to the Volturno River. Dutch then went to Ireland and then to England from which they were dropped into Normandy in the early hours of June 6, 1944. Dutch had his helmet shot off, took two prisoners and got shot in the leg.

Dutch next jumped into Holland on September 17, 1944. His best friend was killed right next to him. He went through the Battle of the Bugle and crossed the Elbe River into Germany where the division met the Russians. After the war Dutch began working in construction. He married in 1946 and had two daughters who gave him three grandsons. All of their wedding dresses were made from one of Dutch's old white parachutes.

[1] Died after parachute jump Fayetteville, Nc.

Profile

Ed Manley
101st Airborne Div., 502 Parachute Infantry Reg.
WW2 combat jumps in Normandy and Holland
Rifleman
Born: November 5, 1921 in New Jersey Age 72 (1994)
Address: Briney Breezes, Florida

Ed volunteered for the paratroops on January 26, 1942. He took his basic training at Camp Wheeler and Parachute School at Ft. Benning, GA. He was assigned to the 502nd which was joined by the 501st and 506th Parachute Infantry Regiments at Ft. Bragg to become the 101st Airborne Division. The division left from Camp Shanks, NJ to England on the HMS Strathmauer and the Erickson.

Ed jumped at 1:25AM June 6th into Normandy and landed eight miles from the intended drop zone. It took him three days to find the 502. On September 17, 1944 Ed jumped into Holland where the 502 had to reinforce the 3rd battalion in a major battle at Best. On September 17, 1944 the division was trucked to Bastogne, Belgium where they were surrounded by the Germans in the Battle of the Bulge. Ed was wounded in the legs by four Mark IV tanks that wiped out D and F companies to only 22 men left. If you couldn't walk you were shot. Ed was taken to POW camp Stalag XII near Limburg, Germany where he lost 44 pounds in three months. The POWs were put on a train which was strafed by our fighter aircraft during which time Ed and five other POWs escaped. They lost one man crossing into the American lines.

On returning to the U.S. Ed was sent to Thayer General Hospital in Ashville, NC from which he was discharged on October 26, 1945.

Profile ★

Rene Dussaq
101st Airborne Div., 502nd Parachute Infantry Reg.
WW2 combat jumps in France
Special Forces Officer Liaison and Intelligence
Born: May 6, 1911 Age 82 (1994) **Died**: June 5, 1996
Address: Encino, CA

Rene was born in Argentina, and educated in Argentina, Switzerland, and Cuba. He came to the U.S. where he became a stuntman in Hollywood from 1932 to 1934, then joined the famed John Craigs Adventure Team as a deep sea diver for the feature "Danger is my Business" from 1935 to 1939. He taught Geopolitics as a visiting lecturer in colleges and universities from 1939 to 1941. Following Pearl Harbor he volunteered for the U.S. Army Paratroops. At Ft. Benning, GA, Rene was selected to be an instructor at the school and went to OCS and later became commanding officer of a unit of the 87th Light Mountain Infantry Division at Camp Hale, CO. He served with the office of strategic services in France and Germany as a member of a 'Jedburgh Team,' and was awarded the Distinguished Service Cross for extraordinary heroism against the enemy. In a verification report by Lt. G.A. Schriever, Dec.4, 1944, it was stated that Rene Dussaq was instrumental in taking of the French city of Thiers, France by having delivered an ultimatum to the Germans in the name of an "American Army" when he actually was alone. He also, by a similar ruse, succeeded in effecting the surrender of a German garrison of about 500 in the town of Issoire (Puy de Dome).

Profile ★

Rollie Duff
82nd Airborne Div., 507th Parachute Infantry Reg.
WW2 combat jumps Normandy & Rhine River
Radio Operator/Path Finders
Born: September 5, 1915 Age 78 (1994) **Died** : May7, 1995
Address: Ft. Myers Beach, FL

Rollie served in communications platoon Headquarters 2nd Btn as radio operator for Colonel Charles Timms while in training. While in Portrush, Ireland Rollie volunteered as a Pathfinder for Normandy invasion. Pathfinders jump prior to the later main parachute drop to set up communications and identify the drop zones. Rollies team left a British base in North Witham, England about 9:30PM on June 5th and dropped between the Merdet River and La Diere bridge at 11:30PM. They were engaged by the enemy immediately and suffered heavy losses however they were able to set up their communications equipment under cover of the remaining men. They were later commended by the 9th Troop Carrier Command as having provided the signal for guiding the aircraft of General James Gavin, commander of the 82nd AB Division, to the drop zone. After the main body of troopers landed, the remaining pathfinders fought with their regiment. Rollie was wounded on the 12th day and returned to England.

After recovering, he returned to duty as a pathfinder serving in Chartes, France and Bastogne, Belgium. He dropped across the Rhine River to set up guidance markings and communications for the main body of Operation Varsity airborne troops that followed.

Rollie died May 7, 1995 while parachuting near Moscow, Russia. The jump was to celebrate the Russian 50th Anniversary of their VE Day.

Profile

William (Bill)Priest
101st Airborne Div., 502th Parachute Infantry Reg.
WW2 combat jumps in Normandy /Holland
Rifleman
Born March 7, 1924 Age 69 (1994)
Address: St.Petersburg, FL

Bill and about 20 men parachuted into Normandy about midnight June 5th, 1944 onto a mined sand dune area. After wandering most of the night he was reunited with others of his division who also were dropped in the area. In September 1944 Bill made his second combat jump, into Holland as part of Operation Market Garden. After 72 days on line in Holland the division returned to France for a short rest following which they were taken to Bastogne in trucks for the Battle of the Bulge, In addition to the Germans who surrounded Bastogne, and repeatedly attacked the division lines, the men of the 101st had to deal with the snow and freezing cold of the Ardennes winter.

Bill went back to Long Island, NY after the war to a job at American Express. He later worked 28 years for the city of NY as a junior mechanical engineer. He and his wife Joan had six children. In 1982 he retired on Snell Isle in St. Petersburg, FL.

Profile

Thomas (Tom) Rice
101st Airborne Div., 501st Parachute Infantry Reg.
WW2 combat jumps Normandy & Holland
Staff Sergeant Squad Leader
Born: August 15, 1921 Age 72 (1994)
Address: San Diego, CA

Tom volunteered for the airborne in 1941 after graduating from Coronado High School, San Diego. After Parachute Training at Ft. Benning, GA he was sent to England where he trained with the 101st AB Division. When D-Day was initiated in June of 1944, Tom was in charge of his aircraft and scheduled as the first man out. Although a large calibre gun shot a hole through his chute, Tom landed safely. His division returned to England where it was re-equipted and prepared for the Holland invasion in September. After 72 days on line following that jump, and a short rest, he was with his unit when it was rushed to Bastogne to stop the German break through. He was wounded four times all together, thus placing him high on the list for returning home.

Tom returned home for Christmas in 1945. He graduated from San Diego College/University in 1950 and began his teaching and coaching career.

Profile

Emmert Parmley
101st Airborne Div., 502nd Parachute Infantry Reg.
WW2 combat jumps in Normandy and Holland
Born: June 18, 1923 Age 70 (1994)
Address: Antich, CA

Emmert was wounded in Normandy and nursed back to health by his sister, Lt. Johnny Trotta, in England. He was wounded in Holland and rejoined his unit in March 1945 after he was discharged from the hospital.

Emmert married his high school sweetheart in December 1945 and they had four children. He retired after 34 years with PG&E Utility Company.

Profile

William (Bill) Coleman
101st Airborne Div., 506 Parachute Infantry Reg.
WW2 combat jump Normandy
Communications Specialist
Born: January 21, 1924 Age 70 (1994)
Address: Orlando, FL

Bills' army basic training was at Camp Wheeler, Georgia, followed by communications and jump school at Ft. Benning. Went by libery ship to Ireland and assigned to 101st Abn.

On the night of June 6, 1944 he parachuted into the darkness over Normandy, and was hit in both legs while still in the air. After about five days he and several others were taken prisoner and sent to Limberg, German Camp X11-A. Many prisoners were killed or wounded after being strafed and bombed on roads and trains en route to Germany. Later transfered to Stalag 1V-B and Arbeits Dienst 1311 in Dresden. When the war ended Bill returned home on the U.S.S. Bittner

Bill graduated from Northwestern U. with a BA in business, and from Crummer School of Business at Rollins with a masters in business.

Bill spent a lifetime in Central Florida in Civic, political and business pursuits, primarily in real estate as developer and broker.

He is a former member of the State Legislature and was Floridas' first Secretary of transportation. He was a Vice President of Days Inns and Commissioner of the S.S. GSA from 1989 to 1993, where he was responsible for all the government real estate, managing an eight billion dollar budget and 10,000 employees

Profile ★

Richard (Teddy) Tedeschi
82nd Airborne Div., 505th Parachute Infantry Reg.
WW2 combat jumps in Italy, Normandy & Holland
Machine Gunner
Born: Sept. 28, 1921 N.Y. City, Age 73 (1994)**Died:**March 1,1999
Address: Bronx, NY

Richard went through basic training at Camp Croft, S.C. where became friends with Rene Dussaq. From Camp Croft Richard went to Ft. Benning, GA., and paratrooper training then assigned to the 82nd Abn 505th PRI as a machine gunner and BAR man. From there he went to Ft. Bragg, N.C. then to Casablanca, North Africa. Then on to Tunisia on July 9, 1943 for the Sicily jump, where the 504th PIR lost 26 airborne planes due to our own naval fire. After 26 days combat in Sicily, Tedeschi was assigned by General Gavin to jeep recon patrol as he spoke Italian. He shot up a German cycle patrol for which he got the bronze star. From Sicily he made a night jump with the 82nd at Salerno, Italy to aid the British 6th Infantry, pinned down on the beach. He went into Naples with the 82nd when they stopped the German breakthrough at the Volturno River.

He jumped into Normandy on June 6th 1944 with the 505th PRI. He landed just north of St. Mere Eglise. He also jumped into Holland for his fourth combat jump on Sept. 17, 1944. Following the successful assault on the bridge at Nijmegen, where he was wounded, he was sent back to England and then to the U.S.

Richard had a brother Jack who saw combat as a paratrooper with the 82nd Abn 307th engineers. Jack was wounded in Italy, Normandy, and the Battle of the Bulge.

Profile

William (Bill) Sykes
6th British Airborne Div., 7th Btn. Parachute Infantry
WW2 combat jump in Normandy
Sergeant Infantry
Born: December 14, 1925 in England Age 68 (1994)
Address: Long Beach, CA

Bill served with the British armed forces from 1942 to 1949. He parachuted into Normandy the night of June 6th, 1944. German forces captured him in the vicinity of Pont l' Vecque on June 19, following which he was sent to a POW camp in Eastern Germany. In April 1945, with the Russian forces on the eastern bank of the Elbe river and the American forces on the west bank of the Mulde, during a march south he escaped in Wesdorf. He was hidden and sheltered by a family named 'Herman' until the American forces were contacted and he was evacuated to a hospital in England.

In 1962 Bill and his family emigrated to the United States and became American citizens. He graduated as a mechanical engineer and was employed by the British and American Aerospace Industries, retiring from MacDonald Douglas Aircraft Corporation after 20 years service.

Profile ★

Frederick Bailey
6th British Airborne Div., 7th Btn Parachute Infantry
WW2 combat jumps in Normandy and Wesel Germany (Rhine)
Rifleman
Born: 1925 in England, Age 69 (1994) **Died:** April 18, 2001Address: Marlow Bucks, England

Fred parachuted into Normandy with the 6th British Airborne Division at Benouville west of Pegasus bridge to protect the left flank of the beach landings. He was 19 years old at the time and 50 years later he is still in very good health and an active parachutist, even doing free-fall. Fred is a life member of the Royal British Legion, the Airborne Brotherhood and the holder of 5 service medals including a special commendation from the Queen.

Profile

Earl Draper Jr.
509th Parachute Infantry Reg.
WW2 combat jump in S. France
Rifleman
Born: May 23, 1924 Boston, Age 70 (1994)
Address: Inverness, FL

Earl was an avid football player in high school, joined the National Guard at fifteen. In late 1942 he volunteered for Ft. Benning jump school. A year later he found his self in Naples, Italy where he was assigned to the 509th Parachute Infantry. He jumped into Southern France on August 15, 1944, and fought in the mountains north of Nice. He was wounded on September 23, '44. He continued with the 509th into northern France where they joined with the 82nd Division in the Battle of the Bulge. After a month of combat the 509th was reduced to only 48 men, the unit was deactivated and Earl was transfered to the 508th, which he stayed with till the end of the war. He earned two purple hearts and two bronze stars.

Earl stayed in the army for 13 years, during which time he made 41 jumps and then retired as a SFC. As of last count he has four children and nine grandchildren.

Profile ★

Emile Gueguen
WW2 French Resistance
Col. (Ret.) French Paratroops
Born: February 15, 1925 Age 69 (1994) **Died February 14, 2003**
Address: Lajolla, CA

As a teenager Emile grew up in German occupied France under the thumb of the enemy and the Nazi Swastika. At the age of fourteen he saw his country over run and defeated. Soon that after he became active in the French Resistance, keeping alive the hope that someday his country would be free again.

Emile later served with the French paratroopers in the Vietnam war and other areas of Asia, retiring as a Colonel, Comander of the French Legion of Honor, a much decorated Airborne veteran with multiple Croix de Guerres. (French Silver Stars)

A French citizen residing with his wife in San Diego, California. Emile and his close friends, Colonel Pierre and Yvette Collard of Baron-sur-Odon, France, were responsable for the RTN's close working relationship with the French. Through them we obtained transportation, housing, and financial help that made the memorial trip possible, and very enjoyable.

On October 15, 1996 in Paris France, Colonel Emile Gueguen was elevated to the position of Grand Officer of the Legion of Honor by the President of France, Jacques Chirac.

Profile

Howard Greenberg
11th Airborne Div., 541st Parachute Infantry Reg.
WW2 jump in Sandai, Japan
Medic, T5
Born: December 17, 1924 Pittsburgh, Age 69 (1994)
Address: Bay Village, OH

He graduated from high school in May 1942 and then began college in June 1942. He registered for the draft in December 1942 and then went into the army in May 1943 after completing his first year of college. After completing basic training as a medic he was assigned to the 69th Division at Camp Shelby, Mississippi.

From the 69th Howard volunteered for paratroopers jump school. He graduated at Ft. Benning, GA in September 1944. After advanced training he was sent to the Philippines with 541st Parachute Infantry in May 1945, and used as replacements for the 11th Airborne Division. The 11th Airborne had already been involved in the capture of most of the Philippines including Manila. After dropping of the atom bombs, the 11th Airborne Division was the first to enter Japan.

Howard was assigned as a medic to the 511th Parachute Infantry, which was an advanced battalion strength party (about 900 men), that landed at Atsugi Airfield, Japan four days before the signing of the peace treaty with Japan. This unit helped set up General McArthurs headquarters in Tokyo.

Howard was discharged on February 17, 1946 following which he immediately started back to college under the GI bill. He received a Doctorate of Optometry from PA State College in June 1949. He practised Optometry in Lorain, OH for almost 40 years.

(Howard was on the Russian jump plane with Rollie Duff.)

Profile

Everett Hall
509th Parachute Infantry Reg.
WW2 combat jumps (4) in S. France
Medic
Born: March 26,1919 in Ireland, Age 74 (1994)
Address: N. Kingston, RI

Everett was drafted in June 1941 and sent to Camp Lee, VA. where he and 20 other men were selected to be the first medical unit in the paratroopers. He qualified in parachute school in November 1941 and was sent to Ft. Bragg, N.C. where a new parachute camp was opened. In May 1942 Everett made the maiden voyage to Scotland on the unescorted Queen Elizabeth in the record time of five days. They were settled in Hungerford, England and from there made the longest flight ever made in C47s to Oran, N. Africa. From there they jumped onto the French (Vichy) Naval Air Base. Five days later they flew to National Airport, Algiers from where, one week later, jumped in Tunisia. They left N. Africa for Sicily in September 1943 and later the same month jumped in Italy where they spent 21 days in enemy territory. Everett made a boat landing in Anzio in January 1944. On August 15, 1944 he parachuted into S. France and in December 1944 was sent to the Battle of the Bulge. In February 1945 the 509th was broken up as they could not get replacements. Most of the 509 men went to the 82nd AB Div. Everett was the first medic paratrooper to receive the Silver Star medal award. He was also awarded the Soldiers Medal in September 1943 in southern France.

Profile

Elsworth Harger
517th Parachute Infantry Reg.
WW2 combat jump in S. France
Squad Leader (USPA D license, 885 jumps)
Born: October 18, 1924 in Midland MI, Age 69 (1994)
Address: Munising, MI

Born on a small farm near Midland, Michigan, Elsworth volunteered for the paratroops and served from October 1942 until October 1945. He graduated from parachute school in Ft. Benning, GA on September 10, 1943. He was assigned to the 517th Parachute Infantry Regiment which consisted of the 460th Parachute Field Artillery Btn. and the 596th Parachute Engineering Co. The 517th left for Italy in May 1944 and participated in five campaigns; Rome-Amo in Italy, a combat jump into southern France in August 1944, the Battle of the Bulge, Belgium, the Rhineland and Central Europe.

Following the war Elsworth received a B.S. degree in Zoology from Michigan State College. From 1949 until retirement he worked for the Michigan Department of Natural Resources as a Biologist in Wildlife Management.

In 1983 Elsworth began sport parachuting. He is a member of the U.S. Parachute Association, holds a D license and has made over 885 jumps, 853 of which were free-falls.

Elsworth is married and has three sons and three daughters, eight grandchildren, one great grandson.

Profile ★

Lee Hulett
517th Parachute Infantry Reg.
WW2 combat jump in S. France
Demolition Specialist
Born: November 24, 1924 Columbus, OH Age 69 (1994)
Address: Columbia, MD **Died**: October 1, 1995

Lee as a military dependent, was at Schofield Barracks, Oahu during the attach on Pearl on December 7th, 1941. Following parachute school at Ft. Benning, GA he was assigned to the 517th PIR From Ft. Benning, to Toccoa, to Ft.Bragg, N.C. and then made the jump into Southern France on August 15, 1944. After VE day he volunteered for the Pacific theater, and found himself two weeks later halfway to New York on VJ Day. Upon arriving in the states he was discharged with 40% disability. Lee attended Oregon State University and during the summer of 1946,47 and 48 was on their National Championship Swim team. He continued parachuting and became a USPA certified jumpmaster with over 1000 jumps when he joined our Return To Normandy Assoc. He was well on his way to becoming a member of the small prestigious BASE jumping group which has as its requirement jumps from a Bridge, Antenna, Skyscraper and Earth formation such as a mountain. Lee had only the building jump to complete when he was killed in a parachuting accident on October 1, 1995 at Hanover, PA at the age of 70. He had over 1400 jumps to his credit at the time of his death. Lee still had his original WW2 jumpsuit and boots that he wore on demo jumps along with a WW2 paratrooper jump helmet complete with chin strap.

Lee was married twice from which he had six children and ten grandchildren.

Profile

Ken Kasse
17th Airborne Div.,
WW2 combat jump at Rhine River
Rifleman
Born: July 27, 1925 in Sellersburg. IN Age 68 (1994)
Address: Perrysville, OH

Kenneth was drafted on November 10, 1943. He trained at Camp Shelby, Miss. with the 65th Infantry Division and then volunteered for the paratroops. In November 1944 he completed Parachute School in Ft. Benning, GA. then boarded the Queen Elizabeth for France. He joined the 17th AB Div., 513th PIR in Sur-Moure, France then jumped across the Rhine river near Wesel, Germany on March 24th, 1945. He was honored to march in the victory parade with the 82nd AB Division in New York in January 1946.

Kenneth is married with three grandchildren and had three brothers who served in WW2.

Profile

Warren LeVangia
82nd Airborne Div., 504th Parachute Infantry Reg.
WW2 combat jumps in Italy
Staff Sergeant Platoon Leader
Born: January 27, 1922 in Lynn MA, Age 71 (1994)
Address: Vergennes, VT

In February 1940 Warren joined a National Guard unit which was called to active duty in January 1941 and sent to Camp Edwards, MA. In 1942 Warren volunteered for the paratroopers and was sent to Camp Croft, S.C. for basic training and then to Ft. Benning, GA where he graduated from Parachute School in June 1942.

He was assigned to "D" Co. of the 504th PIR and made his first combat jump in the Sicilian invasion wherein 23 of our C-47 paratroop aircraft were shot down by the might of our own Allied and enemy fire.

Warren returned to Africa and then back to Sicily at Trapani to make a second combat jump at the Salerno Beachhead. The 504th then fought as infantry to Naples, then to hill 1205 near Casino. From there a return to Puzzouli, near Naples to board ships for the Anzio beach. A "D" Co. attack on Borgo Piava was repulsed by German tanks. Eight men were captured including Warren.

Warren spent 15 months in Stalag Luft 6 and 4 near Nurenburg and after a 90 mile walk to Mooseburg, Bavaria in February 1945 he was liberated by the American 14th Armored Div. at Kriegsgefanganen Lager on April 29, 1945. He saw the infamous Dachau Camp two days after it was liberated and 'knew what we were fighting for.' Trade, watchmaker, married 49 years.

Profile

Richard Mascuch
551st Parachute Infantry Reg.
WW2 combat jump in S. France
First Lieutenant
Born: February 8, 1920 Age 73 (1994)
Address: Morristown, NJ

Richard served in the Army from May 1941 until September 1945. He graduated from Parachute School in Ft. Benning, GA on November 28, 1942. He served in the Mediterranean and European theaters and jumped into southern France in August 1944. He was honorably discharged on November 27, 1945.

He is an active skydiver with over 290 jumps. In 1983 he retired as president from Breeze Corporation. Inc. (now Technology Corp.) and is a director of the company. He married his wife Olga in 1943.

Profile

Richard (Dick) Mandich
101st Airborne Div., 506th Parachute Infantry Reg.
WW2 combat jump in Holland
Radio Operator
Born: December 17, 1924 Age 69 (1994)
Address: San Diego, CA

Dick born in Bessemer, PA volunteered at 18 into the Ski Troops. Sent to Camp Hale, CO., in September 1943 where he trained with the mountain infantry, later enlised in the paratroops and trained at Ft. Benning, GA. On September 17, 1944 he took off for Holland and jumped near Eindhoven. His aircraft was hit several times and was on fire when they exited. For awhile their lines were on both sides of the north/south highway which were held while our Allied forces drove north under our cover, named "Hells Highway".

After 72 days on line was moved to Joigny, France for 16 days of rest when word came of a major German offensive in the Ardennes area in what came to be known as the Battle of the Bulge. The 101st Airborne Division was rushed to the area in open trucks in freezing weather and men were packed in like cattle. On Dec. 19th moved into Bastogne and the next day were encircled by the Germans who were driven back. In April saw combat in the Ruhr area, then on to Landsberg and across southern Germany through Munich to Berchesgaden. On Dec. 11th boarded the Queen Mary for home and on January 19th, 1946 was discharged at Ft. McArthur in San Pedro, CA.

Dick graduated with a degree in Electrical Engineering in 1951, and retired in 1989 after 37 years as an engineer. He and wife Ina had four sons.

Profile

Thomas Zouzas
82nd Airborne Div., 504th Parachute Infantry Reg.
WW2 combat jump in Holland
Intelligence
Born: September 19, 1920 Age 73 (1994)
Adress: Ellsworth, KS

Thomas went to Kansas State College where he was in all sports but was best in football. He volunteered for the paratroops during WW2 and in early 1943 completed Parachute School in Ft. Benning, GA. He was in the army 3 years. He landed in Casablanca, North Africa in early 1943 as a replacement then went to Naples, Italy. His 504th regiment was left in Italy to invade Anzio whilte the rest of the 82nd Airborne sailed to England to prepare for the invasion in Europe. Tom parachuted into Grave, Holland as part of the Operation Market campaign on September 17, 1944. He was discharged in December 1945.

Tom and his wife Christine have 2 boys, 2 girls and 7 grandchildren. He retired in 1982 from United Technologies .

Profile

John Dunn
82nd Airborne Div., 504th Parachute Infantry Reg.
WWII combat service as a Medic.
Born: September 26, 1925 Age 68 (1994)
Address: Brookfield, Wisconsin

John joined the Army in 1944, volunteered for the paratroops, completed jump school and then received training as a medic. He served in Europe with the 504th PIR, 3rd Btn and saw action in Holland, Belgium and Germany. John completed a residency program at the National College of Chiropractic and has since treated many children with spinal deformities. He fought for the 135 pound championship of the Golden gloves and resumed parachuting at age 60. John has three children and four grandchildren and has become proficient at playing the bagpipes.

Profile ★

John (Chinook) Onder
17th Airborne Div., 466th FA Battalion
WW2 combat jump in Wesel, Germany
Machine Gunner
Born: January 13, 1922 Age 71 (1994) **Died:** July 2000[3]
Address: Edison, NJ

John was inducted into the army in November 1942 and discharged in January 1946. He completed parachute training at Ft. Benning, GA in August 1943 and then trained at Camp McKall, NC with the 17th Airborne Division. He participated in the Battle of the Bulge, Ardennes, Rhineland and Central European campaigns.

John marched in the Victory parade up 5th Avenue, NY with the 82nd Airborne Division on January 12, 1946. He remained a bachelor and retired in 1980 after 25 years with Edison Fire Department.

[3] Natural cause

Profile ★

Ernest Raxter
101st Airborne Div., 506th Parachute Infantry Reg.
WW2 combat jump in Holland
Staff Sergeant Instrument Maintenance
Born: May 6, 1922 in Murphy, NC Age 71 (1944)
Died: November 19, 1996
Address: Athens, TX

Ernest entered the army at Houston, Texas from there he went to Ft. Hood and on to Camp Roberts, CA for his basic training. He joined the Airborne and was sent to Parachute School at Ft. Benning, GA., and from there he went to Ft. Bragg, NC and on to Ramsbury, England. On September 17, 1944 he jumped into Holland in the Operation Market Garden operation. After Holland his unit was sent to Bastogne where they participated in the seige of Bastogne and the Battle of the Bulge.

He was the recipient of the Purple Heart.

He retired in 1968 from the Army, then worked in Civil Service as an instructor at an armored school. In 1989 he retired after 20 years. His wife Ruth passed away in 1992.

Profile

Durward Lee (Swede) Reyman
11th Airborne Div., 188th Parachute Infantry Reg.
WW2 jump in Luzon
S/Sgt Squad Leader
Born: October 7, 1923 in Hartley, IA Age 70 (1994)
Address: Ft. Morgan. CO

Swede enlisted in the Army Air Corps. After a number of assigments he was sent to Camp Luna, Las Vegas, NV as drill instructor and sub-machine gun instructor. After a few months he volunteered for Artic Search and Rescue duty and was sent to Wisconsin and Maine for training. After driving sled dogs for a year in Northern Quebec, Canada he volunteered for the paratroopers. After completing Jump School at Ft. Benning, GA he was sent to the Pacific theater where he made a jump on Luzon, Phillipines in July 1945.

After the two A Bombs were dropped and the surrender of Japan in August 1945, his 3rd battalion was sent to Japan and arrived at Atsugi, Airfield the same day General MacArthur did. Swede came back to the U.S. and was discharged on January 16, 1946.

(Swede was on the Russian jump plane with Rollie Duff.)

Profile

James Ruzzuto
82nd Airborne Div., 508th Parachute Infantry Reg.
WW2 combat jump in Holland
Automatic Rifleman
Born: November 10, 1924 in Monessen, PA Age 69 (1994)
Address: Waterford, MI

Jim was drafted into the 75th Infantry Division in 1943. He volunteered for the airborne and after completing parachute school, joined the 82nd AB Div., 508th PIR in Nottingham, England. He jumped into Holland on September 17, 1944 where he was taken prisoner and later liberated by the Russians on April 29, 1945.

Jim is married and has one daughter and one grandson.

Profile

Al Sepulveda
17th Airborne Div., 193 Hqls
WW2 combat jumps in Holland & Rhine River
Rifleman
Born: 1921 Age 73 (1994)
Address: Imperial Beach, CA

Al volunteered for the Airborne and completed parachute training at Ft. Benning, GA in 1944. He left for Europe in August and parachuted into Holland on September 17, 1944 with the 101st AB Div. in Operation Market Garden, the invasion of German occupied Holland. After 72 days and a short rest he was rushed into the Battle of the Bulge, where the men had to contend with snow and bitter cold in the Ardennes. Evacuated, Al was sent to a hospital in England with frostbite where he stayed 49 days. Initially there was concern that he would lose his feet. Upon leaving the hospital he was sent to the 17th AB Div. and took part in Operation Varsity, the drop across the Rhine near Wesel Germany on March 24, 1945. When the European war was over May 1945, Al volunteered for the war against Japan. The war ended before he arrived in Japan, so he was sent to Ft. MacArthur in San Pedro for discharge in September 1945.

Profile

Kelly Stumpus
101st Airborne Div., 907th FA Battalion
WW2 combat jump in Holland
Captian, Artillery Liaison
Born: December 7, 1919 in Boston, Age 74 (1994)
Address: Pasadena, CA

Kelly attended UCLA before he was inducted as a $21 amonth draftee on November 5, 1941. He joined the 101st Airborne Division as a replacement after the Normandy invasion in August 1944. He parachuted into Holland as a member of the 907th Glider Field Artillery Battalion of the 501st combat team on September 17. His duties were that of an observer from an artillery liaison Piper Cub airplane during their 73 days in Holland.

During the Bastogne campaign Kelly was the liaison with the 3rd Btn. of the 501st. He was awarded the Air Medal and the Purple Heart. He was discharged in January 1946.

Upon returning to civilian life Kelly completed his accounting eduction at UCLA and later became a CPA. In 1961 he helped organize a commerical laundry equiptment company. The company expanded and did so well with Kelly as president that he was able to retire in 1984.

Kelly made commemorative anniversary jumps, 40th\45th in Holland in 1984 and 1989, and is past president of the 101st Airborne Division Association 1988-1989.

Profile ★

Ken Shaker
509th Parachute Infantry Reg.
WW2 combat jump in S. France
Captain, Company Commander
Born: 1916 Age 78 (1994) **Died:** May 3, 2001 (Arlington)
Address: San Diego, CA

In 1932 Ken stowed away on a ship in San Fransico to get to the fighting in Shanghai, but ended up in Singapore. He returned to school but quit after one year of college. He went to Spain in 1937 and spent 18 months in active combat in the Spanish Civil War.

Ken joined the 509th Infantry Regiment in Africa in January 1943, and was in reserve in the Sicily invasion. While on a special mission in the invasion of Italy, his unit of 40 men captured an advanced German radar station and 140 German prisoners and missed capturing Mussolini by 24 hours. He was then in the battle near Monte Casino at Verafro and among the first units to make the landing at the Anzio beach head . Ken jumped into Southern France in 1944 and fought in the mountains north of Nice. Next he took part in the Battle of the Bulge with the 82nd AB Div. After a month of combat the 509th was reduced to 48 men, the unit was deactivated and he was transferred to the 508th PIR.

After the war Ken sold life insurance to military personnel. During this period he landed in Beirut 24 hours after the Marine landing in 1958 and ended up selling to the Marines in their foxholes. He also spent 18 months, including the TET offensive, in Viet Nam as a civilian in 1967 and 1968.

INDEX

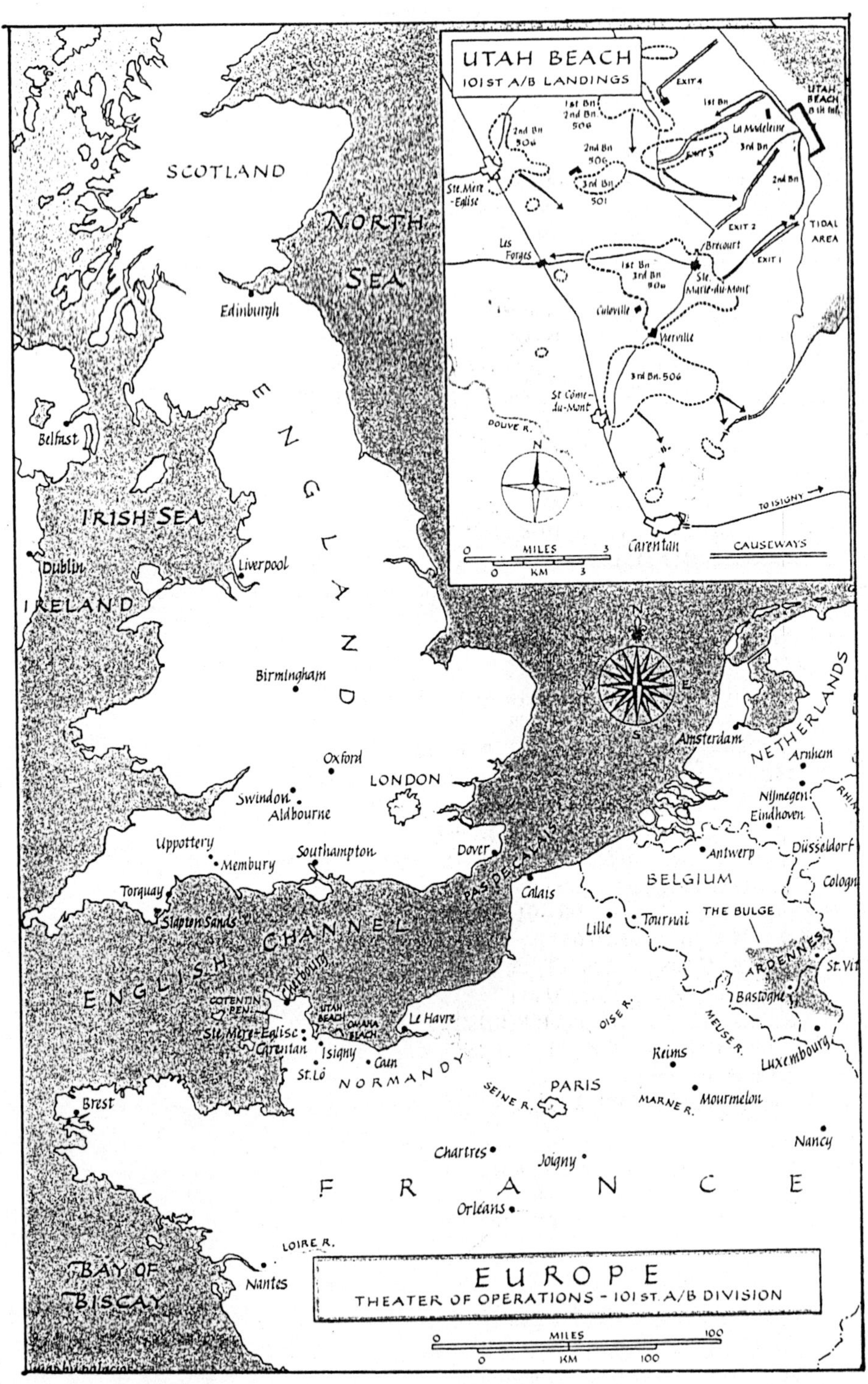
UTAH BEACH
101ST A/B LANDINGS
EUROPE
THEATER OF OPERATIONS - 101 ST. A/B DIVISION
SCOTLAND
NORTH SEA
IRISH SEA
ENGLAND
IRELAND
ENGLISH CHANNEL
BAY OF BISCAY
FRANCE
BELGIUM
NETHERLANDS
NORMANDY
ARDENNES
THE BULGE
PAS DE CALAIS
Edinburgh
Belfast
Dublin
Liverpool
Birmingham
Oxford
LONDON
Swindon
Aldbourne
Uppottery
Membury
Southampton
Dover
Torquay
Slapton Sands
Cherbourg
COTENTIN PEN.
UTAH BEACH
OMAHA BEACH
Ste. Mère-Eglise
Carentan
Isigny
Caen
St. Lô
Le Havre
Brest
Calais
Lille
Tournai
Antwerp
Amsterdam
Arnhem
Nijmegen
Eindhoven
Düsseldorf
Bastogne
Luxembourg
Reims
Mourmelon
PARIS
Chartres
Joigny
Orléans
Nantes
Nancy
LOIRE R.
SEINE R.
OISE R.
MARNE R.
MEUSE R.
MILES
KM
0
100
Ste. Mère-Eglise
Les Forges
Ste. Marie-du-Mont
Brecourt
La Madeleine
Culoville
Vierville
St Côme-du-Mont
Carentan
DOUVE R.
TO ISIGNY
TIDAL AREA
CAUSEWAYS
EXIT 1
EXIT 2
EXIT 3
EXIT 4
1st Bn 2nd Bn 506
2nd Bn 506
3rd Bn 501
1st Bn 3rd Bn 506
3rd Bn. 506
3
N
W
E
S

~ In Memoriam ~

ROLLAND DUFF

1916 - 1995

I know many of you watched our D-Day re-enactment jumps on television June 5, 1994. Do you remember the old guy who unfurled the American flag on the way down? CNN kept their cameras on him a long time, all the way to the ground. His name was Rollie Duff, he was 77 at the time.

He was killed on May 7, 1995, in Moscow, Russia making a parachute jump with the Russians to celebrate their VE Day on the fiftieth anniversary. His chute became tangled on opening, moments later his reserve tangled also, causing him to fall to his death.

We all are aware of the risks we take with every parachute jump because of our advanced ages and brittle bones, also aware of the patriotism that it brings to our children when they would see Rollie and his flag. That is worth the risk to true patriots like Rollie Duff.

My first reaction was one of great sadness for my W.W.II comrade, and one of only nineteen of us that had jumped both in 1944 Normandy invasion and the 1994 re-enactment.

Later I realized Rollie was doing what he wanted to do, having the time of his life and putting it to good use. He was 78 and he passed quickly. His country will think kindly of him. How many of us will fare that well?

In 1944 Rollie volunteered as a Pathfinder for the historic Normandy D-Day and Rhine River (45) jumps, and was among the first to land on enemy soil. He was wounded in France.

They brought Rollie home on Air Force One carrying the President, he would have liked that, followed by a military ceremony at Andrews Air Force Base before burial in Minneapolis.

Rollie was a member of the 507 Parachute Infantry Regiment, 82nd Airborne Division with two combat parachute jumps in W.W.II. He served in the communications platoon of headquarters, 2nd battalion as radio operator for then Colonel Charles Timms while in training. While in Portrush, Ireland, Rollie volunteered as a Pathfinder for the upcoming Normandy invasion. Pathfinders' tasks were to jump before the later main parachute drop to set up communications and to identify the drop zones for pilots.

Rollies' team left a British base at North Witham, England about 9:30 PM on June 5 and dropped between the Meredet River and La Fiere bridge at 11:30 PM. They engaged the enemy immediately and suffered heavy losses, however they were able to set up their communications equipment under cover of the remaining men.

They were commended by the 9th Troop Carrier Command as having provided the signal for guiding the aircraft of General James Gavin, commander of the 82nd AB Division to the drop zone. After the main body of troopers landed, the remaining pathfinders fought with their regiment. Rollie was wounded on the June 12 and returned to England. After recovering, he returned to duty as a pathfinder serving in Chartes, France, and Bastogne, Belgium. He dropped across the Rhine River to set up guidance markings and communications for the main body of Operation Varsity airborne troops that followed.

C-47 Club

82nd A/B Division

~ In Memoriam ~

LEE SANFORD HULETT

1925 - 1995

It was early in September of 1995 that Lee Hulett was featured on CBS 48 Hours for his continued enjoyment of skydiving at age 70. Lee was another member of our Return To Normandy group and you might remember him also, during the re-enactment he was the one that wore the W.W.II steel pot helmet. He also was on the plane with Rollie Duff when Rollie's chute malfunctioned in Russia. (May 1995)

Lee Hulett of Columbia, Maryland died October 1, 1995, in a skydiving accident at Hanover, Pa., on his fourth jump that day. No parachute was deployed. He loved skydiving and said that if he happened to die that way, not to grieve for him. "I will go out with a smile on my face," he said many times, and he did. It was suggested that he had a heart attack, as he was seen grabbing at his chest as he fell to earth. It was also said that he suffered from tendonitis, which might have made it difficult to deploy his parachute.

Although he did not jump on D-Day 1944, Lee fought in Italy before jumping in southern France on August 5 of that year, and forty years later belatedly received the Bronze Star.

"He was full-throttle all the way," said his son Lee Jr., "He went the way he wanted."

517th P.I.R.

VOIE DE LA LIBERTY

or way of the freedom, is indicated by these markers accross Europe for over eleven hundred miles begining in Normandy, it follows path of the conquering Third Army

"It Has Always Been The Soldier"

"It is the soldier, not the reporter Who
has given us freedom of the press;

It is the soldier, not the poet Who has
given us
freedom of speech;

It is the soldier, not the campus
organizer Who has given us
freedom to demonstrate;

It is the soldier Who salutes the flag;
Who serves beneath the flag;
And whose coffin is draped by the flag,
Who allows the protester to burn the flag."

(Anon)

Ste Mère Église, Normandy

U.S. AIRBORNE
Interesting Facts & Statistics Of D-Day

From thirteen airfields across England, 801 U.S. C-47 Skytrain aircraft took off for Normandy loaded with 13,400 U.S. Paratroopers of the 101st and 82nd Airborne Divisions late in the evening of June 5, 1944. They stretched nine across and three hundred miles long flying just five hundred feet above the waters of the English Channel This was followed by four missions on June 6th starting before dawn of 313 more C-47's towing U.S. CG-4A and British Horsas gliders carrying 1792 troops, 215 vehicles, 75 pieces of artillery, and 174 tons of cargo (mostly ammunition).

The 506th Parachute Regiment of the 101st Airborne Division was transported by 116 C-47s of the 439th and 435th Troop Carrier Groups. Aircraft losses on the flights carrying the 506th were six lost, and twenty seven damaged.

One aircraft (chalk no. 49) of this group is presently on display in the Airborne museum at St. Mere Eglise, and has been repainted to look like the Argonia, the lead plane flown by Col Charles H. Young. It was the plane next to mine (48) in the formation and carried my good buddies Otto Sykes and Richard Falvey.

It is estimated 291 men of the 101st Airborne Division were killed in action the first twenty four hours, with total causalities of ten percent.

With revisionist in mind, and repeatedly questioned by historians, I feel obligated to include the following: This Airborne combat operation consisted mainly of male caucasians with some Native-Americans, Asian-Americans, and Latinos. There were no African-American or female troops involved.

AIRBORNE
British Statistics Of D-Day

From British bases 237 aircraft, many of them C-47s took off simultaneously loaded with 4,255 British Paratroopers of the 6th Airborne Division, destination Lower Normandy northeast of Caen, near the city of Ranville.

Preceding this large formation by one hour was six Halifax aircraft fromTarrant Rushton, Dorset towing six Horsa gliders at an altitude of six thousand feet. These carried the first British combat troops to go into action in France, 150 men led by Major John Howard, and was the most successful operation of the invasion.

With three platoons from D Company of the Oxford and Buckinghamshire Light Infantry Regiment (Ox and Bucks), Major Howard landed by glider soon after midnight beside the Orne Canal bridge, and captured it intact. Minutes later two other platoons that had landed close to the Orne River bridge five hundred yards away captured it intact.

By 0021 hours, June 6, D company had taken its objectives. Minute accounts of this raid and the successful capture of the bridges can be found in the book, Pegasus Bridge.

-o-

About D-Day June 6, 1944

"The most difficult and complicated operation ever to take place."

Winston Churchill

"The destruction of the enemy's landing is the sole decisive factor in the whole conduct of the war and hence in its final results."

Adolf Hitler

"The history of war does not know of an undertaking comparable to it for the breadth of conception, grandeur of scale, and mastery of execution."

Joseph Stalin

"Good Luck! And let us all beseech the blessing of Almighty God upon this great and noble undertaking."

Dwight D. Eisenhower

"In this column I want to tell you what the opening of the second front entailed, so that you can know and appreciate and forever be humbly grateful to those both dead and alive who did it for you."

Ernie Pyle

~ Recommended ~
Books & Films about D-Day June 6, 1944

Ridgeway's Paratroopers, *by Clay Blair*
ISBN 0-385-27888-8

D-Day June 6, 1944, *by Stephen E. Ambrose*
ISBN 0-671-67334-3

Band Of Brothers, *by Stephen E. Ambrose*
ISBN 0-671-86736-9

The 101st Airborne At Normandy, *by Mark A. Bando*
ISBN 0-87938-873-0

Into The Valley, *by Col. Charles H. Young*
ISBN 0-9647978-0-1

D-Day With The Screaming Eagles, *by George Koskimaki*
ISBN 0-689-22784-0

D-Day, *by Richard Collins (British)*
ISBN 1-55859-396-9

The Longest Day, *by Cornelius Ryan*
ISBN 0-671-89091-3

Best Films

The Longest Day, by Darryl F. Zanuck 1961
Saving Private Ryan, *by Stephen Spielberg* 1998
Band of Brothers, *by Tom Hanks, Stephen Spielberg* 2001

Museum

National D-Day Museum, New Orleans, La. 2000

Appendix

It was October 26, 1997 that Jeanine and Andre Mosqueron of Paris, France arrived at the Cincinnati Northern Kentucky International Airport, for an eight day visit to our farm home in Union, Kentucky. They had accepted our invitation. Besides bottles of French wine and chocolates, the Mosquerons brought a picture of a new statue that now stands at la Fiere bridge near the swamps of Amfreville where American Paratroopers landed in 1944 and stopped a column of German tanks from crossing.

A GRATEFUL TRIBUTE
TO AMERICAN AIRBORNE SOLDIERS
OF "D.DAY"
6 JUNE 1944 ~ 7 JUNE 1997

During the Mosquerons visit, I was surprised to learn that both Jeanine and Andre were born in Normandy in 1948, Jeanine seven miles northeast of St Mere Eglise, and just two miles from Foucarville, the place I landed in 1944, Andre just eight miles southeast of Carentan. Jeanines father was my age, born in 1922, and had been sent to Germany to a work camp, escaping shortly before D-Day he went home to Normandy. He had described to Jeanine how on June 6, 1944, still in hiding, he looked out at the confusion, as first a group of German soldiers would pass, then a group of American paratroopers, ...then Germans again.

Also in October 1997 I received a surprise e-mail from Sergeant First Class Joe Shrigley, a former member of 1st Battalion, 10th Special Forces Group from Stuttgart, Germany in 1994. Joe was nearing the end of a five year tour in Germany when his unit was assigned to coordinate and provide all support for our RTN jump. This unit was commanded by Col. McMillan, whose father, Capt. McMillan, I had known and jumped with when he was an officer in my unit on D-Day 1944. For sentimental reasons I had Col. McMillan sign my jump log book as we walked off the field after the re-enactment jump in 1994. Joe provided me with behind the scenes activities in the days before our jump, and about the help the Special Forces gave the RTN men.

The orders to support the RTN jump came on very short notice, after the on again, off again negotiations. It was Joe who had to drive to the French Skydiving Center, Ferte Gaucher, fifty miles east of Paris just the night before our jump to pick up the parachutes the club had offered, after our government said we could not use US Army chutes. Without those chutes, there would have been no jump, ...indeed this book would not have been written.

Again, it seemed like divine guidance to succeed in the face of government opposition, not to mention the terrible weather conditions the days before the jump, changing to blue skies just for our memorial, changing back to rain the following day.

November, 1997 saw the release of another new book by Stephen E. Ambrose.[4] Citizen Soldiers begins in Normandy June 7, 1944, the day after D-Day and takes the reader across Europe to the wars end, May 7, 1945. Must reading for any WWII buff. (He mentions the conference we attended May 7-8, 1995 in New Orleans) Mr. Ambrose died from lung cancer in October 2002.

---

[4] Mr. Ambrose was technical adviser to director Steven Spielberg when making the 1998 movie 'Saving Private Ryan', a wonderful, but very graphic film about the D-Day landings. Also 'Band of Brothers' about our E Company in 2001.

THE NATIONAL D-DAY MUSEUM

NEW ORLEANS

Dedicated June 6, 2000 by World War II historian and author, Stephen E. Ambrose

945 Magazine Street, New Orleans, LA 70130 504-527-6012

www.ddaymuseum.org

On June 5th, at the Hilton Hotel in New Orleans, Steve Ambrose, Steven Spielberg, Tom Hanks, Tom Brokaw, and US Secretary of Defense Wm. Cohen gathered for a day long session of interviews with D-Day veterans.

On June 6th, a huge military parade started at the Super Dome with D-Day veterans riding in trucks and jeeps, and after winding through the downtown streets of New Orleans ended at the Arena, where the museum dedication was held. Late in the afternoon, after D-Day veterans with special passes visited the museum, it was opened to the public. Steve Ambrose, who had worked hard for seven years to make it a reality, admitted it was one of the happiest days of his life.

Photo: David Burnett/Contact Press

Bob Williams rides jeep in parade

***David Burnett,* Contact Press-Photographer, extraordinarie…**

A free-lance photographer on assignment for Time/Life magazines, David lived in Saigon from 1970 to 1972 shooting the horrors of the Vietnam War. Fortunately, he showed up in Normandy in 1994 to capture Bob Williams field of dreams on film for Time magazine. Bob was very happy to meet David in New Orleans for the first time at the grand opening of the National D-Day Museum.

***Mike Griffith*, Middlesex, England, writes…**

"As an Englishman, born after the war (1950), I have a great interest in the history of WWII, especially the D-Day landings. I have always felt that your war was with the Japanese, and had the might of the American Armed Forces and industry been turned solely to them, I am sure you could have defeated them much sooner and with much less loss of lives. But, you chose to come to the aid of a friend in desperate need. I am sure that without your help, we could not have defeated Germany.

I have visited Normandy on several occasions and I always end up at the cemetery at Colleville St. Laurant. It is a place for reflection of sadness and glory. God bless all of them who paid with their lives. And God bless all of them who came and returned home."[5]

[5] The Screaming Eagle-Jan/Feb 2000

Excerpts from Ernie Pyles account of the aftermath of the D-Day invasion.

Normandy Beachhead, June 1944.

I took a walk along the historic coast of Normandy in the country of France.

It was a lovely day for strolling along the seashore. Men were sleeping on the sand, some of them sleeping forever. Men were floating in the water, but they didn't know they were in the water, for they were dead.

I walked for a mile and a half along the water's edge of our many-miled invasion beach. You wanted to walk slowly, for the detail on that beach was infinite.

The wreckage was vast and startling. The awful waste and destruction of war, even aside from the loss of human life, has always been one of its outstanding features to those who are in it. Anything and everything is expendable. And we did expend on our beachhead in Normandy during those first few hours.

For a mile out from the beach there were scores of tanks and trucks and boats that you could no longer see, for they were at the bottom of the water-swamped by overloading, or hit by shells, or sunk by mines. Most of their crews were lost.

On the beach lay, expended, sufficient men and mechanism for a small war. They were gone forever now. And yet we could afford it.

We could afford it because we were on, we had our toehold, and behind us there were such enormous replacements for this wreckage on the beach that you could hardly conceive of their sum total. Men and equipment were flowing from England in such a gigantic stream that it made the waste on the beachhead seem like nothing at all, rcally nothing at all.

War correspondent Ernie Pyle was killed by a Japanese sniper while covering the war in the Pacific in April 1945.

I obtained a copy of Cpl. Douglas Montgomery's (ASN 39187514) diary starting on June 4th, 1944, and his account of Headquarters Company, 2nd Battalion, of the 506th Parachute Infantry Regiment, 101st Airborne Division. Sometimes lying in a foxhole he did not write too plainly, but I think I have succeeded almost 100% to record this young PFC's time spent in combat starting with the invasion of France, then Holland, and the battle of Bastogne, where he was finally wounded on the 8th of February, 1945. Doug was my wire man for our communications platoon. I was the message center chief. Doug's job was to carry two rolls of telephone wire and two sound powered telephones, and run wire between Headquarters Company and the letter Companys, I have refrained from making corrections, or adding to his recording of what happened. Doug died in 2001. -Bob Williams

Douglas Montgomery's Diary

June 5, 1944-Monday, D-Day Minus 'One'

Got fitted with our parachutes and went for a dry run to the waiting airplanes. Found out that we invade tonight sometime. We all have darkened our faces with soot from the tent stoves so our faces will not shine.

Had a send off gathering with 'Gen. Ike,' did not stand in formal formation.

5' o'clock had a large supper, anything we wanted to eat.

Went to the waiting planes and made ready. Everyone was redy to go. Aboard the planes about 8' o'clock and took off for Normandy. When airborn jumpmaster gave everyone a pill to make us all feel happy, and it did. Next stop France.

June 6, 1944-Tuesday, D-Day

Took off from airport and jumped in France, 10 miles *(exaggeration)* from where we should of. Enemy was waiting as they let us have it with machine gun fire. We landed in a swamp where some men drowned. Protection for others. A very moon light night and no wind to speak of. We assembled in small groups and fought our way to beach exit No. 1. Under enemy fire at all times. One machine gun was at the corner of the swamp where our plane drop landed. Sgt. Vacko and Capt Cox and myself had to swim together under that damn machine gun fire to cross the first hedge row. We all made it. Laid in the water the rest of the night untill it started to get light. Sgt. Vacko and myself crawed together to get the kraut with the machine gun, but he was gone.

Forenoon : Fighting delaying action of enemy along route of march harressed by snipers.

Afternoon :Along route of march, engaged by enemy at out skirts of Le Gd Chemin. Enemy using four 88's, machine guns and etc.

Note : First dead we saw was a German on a motorcycle. Went to take his P-38 but thought it was booby trapped. Next one was one of our own up the road towards the beach. Captured two first thing, had to kill one. Had a little action blowing up C.P. where Germans were giving signals. All hand grenades were used up. Next night we slept in a sewer pipe to protect us from enemy fire, was with Henderson when he was wounded.

MIA- Sweeney, Porter, Eckels, Williams L. E., Griffin, McAdams, McClelland, Ervin, Ash, LaRose, Hodgkins, Wingett.

WIA- Caumartin, Jeager, Henderson, McLean, Arrowood.

KIA-Halls, Fountain.

June 7, 1944-Wednesday

Note : Later found out that 'Fountain' killed yesterday, crawed up to an 88 and threw a hand grenade down the barrel while it was still firing. Some guts...he lost his. Called for tank help as action stiffened. Stoney the Indian boy got killed there. The German was also killed by Col. Strayer. All those wounded today was at 'Hell's Corner.' Killed another one here, when hit he jumped high and wiggled a little.

Company moving SW from Vierville, attacked by enemy parachutist from left flank on outskirts of village.

Severe action on Hell's corner. Stoney was killed here, others wounded by shrapnel. Enemy defense turned out to be a duck gallery, along swamp hedgerow...hun's were the ducks.

MIA-(in addition to that of 6th June '44) Mihok, Mayer, Kuntz.

WIA-Susel (back to duty), Choo, Snyder, Houge, Henry, Gabor, Brewer, Kraus, Sheidler, Barron.

KIA- Stoney.

June 8, 1944-Thursday

In reserve at Angoville-av-Plain. Harassed by sniper...eliminated. Had a fox hole dug in an orchard, two Germans lay dead near by, and one of our own. Not from our company. First night sleeping in a fox hole, wasn't too bad. Did it many times back in the states. These damed 'K' rations could be better. The breakfast portion is not too bad. Choo, the Chinese boy killed five before he was wounded, was sent back to England, lucky stiff. Harrassed by snipers-think most of them were French women. Killed them all, even the Germans captured. I didn't do it. Tanks withdrew from our positions, don't know where they went.

MIA-Same (no reports) probably killed on jump night-will get reports later.

KIA-Same

WIA-Same

June 9, 1944-Friday

Moved from Angoville-au-Plain to position approximately one mile NW of Bse Adderville (in defense) North of Carentan, artillary fire on Carentan thoughout the day. Two machine gun squads covering bridge. Plastered Carentan, will probably attack tomorrow morning. Can't see how anything can be left to take. Our mortars just firing, Piggy Porter is having a time for himself, using up ammo like it was going out of style. Enemy bombers came over for the first time, dropped a few but dropped most on their own troops. Don't think they knew where the lines were.

MIA-Mihok, Mayer, Kuntz (all returned to duty-gave up for dead)

WIA-Hardin

ABSK-Albritten

June 10, 1944-Saturday

Still in defenseive position. Artillary continued fire on Carentan. Enemy bombers came over about 2400 hours, dropped loads over scattered areas. Came close. MG's harressed by snipers, and under fire of 88's. Not too much action, just waiting to attack Carentan-our first big city. Understand where ' Institute De Notre Dame ' is located. We are sending out small patrols to keep the enemy busy. Pepper was wounded by a sniper, was hit in the left arm-sent back

to England. Drinking lots of apple cider from the French, also was given some hot course bread, but it was better then K Ration.
WIA-Pepper
MIA-Same

June 11, 1944-Sunday

Company in reserve, artillary continues heavy shelling of Carentan. We're about five miles from Carentan getting ourselves together to move out for the attack. Had a briefing on what to expect. We'er going to attack the city from the north Hi-way. Given lots of ammo. Replaced my Carbine with a '45 ' Tompson. Enemy forces expect to be about 3000, but don't know for sure. Believe most enemy troops are Russians as they don't put up much of a fight before they give up. Found a large German flag and saved part of it. Pounded last night by enemy bombers, they hit our C.P. where the brass were staying. No body was killed or wounded, lucky
MIA-Lt. Sweeny, McAdams (both returned to duty)

June 12, 1944- Monday

Left company reserve area to new position west of Carentan considerable fighting on out skirts. Afternoon, moved west engaged enemy approximatly two miles out- heavy resistance with counter attacks by enemy. Captured one hell of a lot of Germans many of them wearing German crosses. Confusion arose as we didn't know what to do with them all. Ask for Divison for help. Col. Zink was real happy but stern. Caught hell from himas I let one German let his arms down. Lt. Winter torn a iron cross from a captured german for a soveneir. Sgt. Dilworth hit one German in the jaw with rifle butt.
MIA- Same
WIA-Truillo, Loveland, Lt. Lavenson, Webster.

June 13, 1994-Tuesday

Stiff resistance by enemy forces continued from west of Carentan. 'Slow Joe' was killed first thing in the morning when we approched the hi-way. Hit the city limits about 11 :o'clock. Taking this city house by house very heavy resistance by enemy and French. Not too much help from the French. Replaces by more ammo as getting low in the afternoon. Had the city taken over by about 3 o'clock. Captured the priest wine cellar. Was with Jack O'Leary when wounded. He was my fighting partner and drinking buddy.

MIA-Same

WIA-Patterson, O'Leary, Johnson, Cox, Meirndorf, Rybinski

KIA-Slosarzyk

June 14, 1944-Wednesday

Relieved in field by 502, moved to garrison in Carentan. Established patrols to cover certain city blocks. Established road blocks. Billeted in Institue de Notre Dame. Wine and wiskey flowed like water-every body got pretty drunk and caught hell from Lt. Reis as he took command as Capt Cox was wounded yesterday. Was sent out on road block but didn't engage any enemy resistance. There was a heavy explosion just south of us but don't know what it was. Getting a few artillary shells from the Germans but not bad.

MIA-Same

WIA-Morganti, Shaw, Byrd

ABSK-Wygol

June 15, 1944-Thursday

Set up defence positions in Carentan. Anticipation of probable counter attack. Boche continued nightly bombing attacks. Stiffened the road blocks with tanks as support. Laid telephone wire all day from C.P. to road blocks. Walkie-talkies were,nt to reliable as batteries were hard to get. Every day we have been in action the weather has been hot. Makes the dead bloat faster. Our forces are using German PW to pick the dead. Their own and ours. Our dead are not put in the same truck.

MIA-Same

ABSK-Williams R.L., Gathings

June 16, 1944-Friday

Defence situation still remains.

MIA-Same

June 17, 1944-Saturday

Situation remains same

June 18, 1944-Sunday
Situation the same
June 19, 1944-Monday
Situation the same
ABSK-Glenn C. Baker
June 20, 1944-Tuesday
Situation the same
June 21, 1944-Wednesday

Left rest area for frontand relieved 501 in defence situation, nothing happening much, near evening the kruats rained 88' shells at us. A couple dog fights overhead during the day.

MIA-Eckels, Williams L.E., Griffin, McClelland, Ervin, Ash, LaRose, Hodgkins, Wingett, Porter.

WIA-Lebworth

June 22, 1944-Thursday

Still in defence position with deep dug in positions. No active enemy action yet except they plastered us with 88's all night long. We'er using mortars to knock out pigeons from trees. (Hun's the pigeons)

Robert M Bogers	made S/Sgt
Orville W. Robbins	made T/5
Robert L. Mann	made T-4
Maj Horton	tran to 3rd Bn
Lt Sweeney	tran to 1st Bn supply
S/Sgt A.P. Campbell	tran to service co
Capt Hester	tran to regt S-3
Capt Clements to	to Bn Sur

June 23, 1944-Friday

(Where is our air-force) Still in defenceive position not much sturring. Enemy for the first time came over and strafed us from the air. Still letting us have it with mortors and 88 fire. Mortar shells lit in Carentan while Gen. was awarding metals. Few were hurt. Mortars still pounding enemy positions 50 times more than what their letting us have it.

KIA-Portor (MIA to KIA)

MIA-Eckles, Williams L.E., Griffin, LaRose, McClelland, Ervin, Ash, Hodgkins, Wingett.

June 24, 1944-Saturday

Situation the same as 23rd June.

KIA- (to date) Stoney, Halls, Fountain, Slosarczk, Porter, LaRose (MIA to KIA)

WIA- Combs

MIA- (to date) Williams L.E., McCelland, Griffin, (WIA), Wingett (WIA), Hodgkins, Ervin (KIA), Ash, Eckles.

June 25, 1944-Sunday

Situation remains the same, (OPLR in the morning)

WIA to date-

Combs, Lebworth, Morganti, Shaw, Byrd, Patterson, O'Leary, Johnson, Cox, Meirndorf, Rybinski, Webster, Taujille, Lavanson, Loveland, Pepper, Hardin, Caumartin, Jeager, Henderson, McLean, Arrowood, Susel (to duty), Choo, Brewer, Snyder, Houge, Henry, Gabor (to duty), Kraus, Sheilden, Barron.

KIA-to date-

Stoney, Halls Fountain, Slosarczk, Porter, LaRose.

ABSK-to duty, Baker GC.

ABSK- Williams RL, Githings, Albritton, Wugal.

June 26, 1944-Monday

Moved position to the left flank, mortars stayed in same place. Still in defensive position. Bad weather seized all action, alittle art. and mortar fire from both sides.

WIA-Woodcock (lwa) back to duty.

June 27, 1944-Tuesday

Got relieved by the 83rd Division about 4 o'clock in the afternoon. Forced marched to Beamant where trucks awaited to take us to the airborne rest area outside of St Sauveur le Vicomte. Got there about 2 o'clock 28, June in the morning.

June 28, 1944-Wednesday

Quite day. Recieved PX rations for the first time.

June 29, 1944-Thursday

Left rest area near St Sauveur le Vicomte 8 :30 this morning riding trucks. Entered new rest area a couple miles outside Cherbourg.

WIA- Wingett, Griffin, (both MIA to WIA June 6th 1944)

June 30, 1944-Friday

Situation the same, still in rest area, rained some. Went on a rat race. *(long hike)*

July 1, 1944- Saturday

Situation the same.

Kersey to T-5, Wright to Cpl.

July 2, 1944-Sunday

Situation the same, (church today)

Lt Neveles to Capt, Lt Brewer to 1st Lt, Lt Maher to 1st Lt, Lt Baranowski to 1st Lt.

The diary skips from here back to Camp Albourne England , when on August 14, 1944 the regiment was told to get ready for another combat jump. Planned for Paris, then called off, then changed to Belgium, then called off, finally on September 17th, 1944 the Regiment jumped in combat in Holland. Since this book is only about Normandy, I did not feel the need to include all of Doug's diary which ended in Bastogne . - Bob Williams

The Jedburghs of the OSS…

The OSS (Office of Secret Service) was formed by "Wild Bill Donavan" during World War II by orders of Gen. Eisenhower. Under Donavan's leadership was formed a group called the Jedburghs, specially trained to parachute in teams of three into occupied territory to train French and Dutch underground to cause as much havoc for the enemy as possible, to send information on military placements and installations back to England.

The Jedburghs were a group of 290 men, 84 American, the rest British, and the French who had escaped to England.

One of these Americans, Rene Dussaq, had been selected from the 101st ABN Div. for a Jedburgh team, and parachuted into Normandy weeks before the invasion in 1944. Rene was in the Return To Normandy group that jumped in 1994. He can be seen leaving the plane at 3400 feet in the picture just after page 49. His profile is on page 106.